The Augsburg Confession and Its Apology

The Lutheran Confessions Series

Edited by Kenneth Wagener and Robert C. Baker

Scripture quotations are from The Holy Bible, English Standard Version, copyright © 2001 by Crossway Bibles, a division of Good News Publishers. Used by permission. All rights reserved.

Quotations of the Small Catechism are from *Luther's Small Catechism with Explanation,* copyright © 1986, 1991 by Concordia Publishing House.

The quotations from the Augsburg Confession and the Apology of the Augsburg Confession are from *Concordia: The Lutheran Confessions,* copyright © 2005 Concordia Publishing House.

This publication may be available in braille, in large print, or on cassette tape for the visually impaired. Please allow 8 to 12 weeks for delivery. Write to the Library for the Blind, 7550 Watson Rd., St. Louis, MO 63119-4409; call toll-free 1-888-215-2455; or visit the Web site: www.blindmission.org

Manufactured in the United States of America

1 2 3 4 5 6 7 8 9 10   14 13 12 11 10 09 08 07 06 05

Contents

Introduction

The Story of the Augsburg Confession

On January 21, 1530, Emperor Charles V called for a general assembly—an imperial diet—to be held in Augsburg, Germany. Convened to deal with the threat of the Turks to the empire and the Lutheran–Roman Catholic disagreement that was dividing the Church, the assembly was held later that year.

For the assembly, the Lutherans prepared a confession of what they believed and taught on the basis of Holy Scripture. Using previously drafted documents and the guidance of Dr. Martin Luther, Philip Melanchthon, a professor friend and colleague of Luther, wrote the Augsburg Confession in both German and Latin. Dr. Luther did not attend the assembly in Augsburg because he was under the imperial ban. That ban declared he could be killed on sight by anyone. Thus, Luther stayed safely in a castle at Coburg under the protection of the Elector of Saxony.

On behalf of the Lutherans, on June 25, 1530, a layman, Dr. Christian Beyer, read the German version of the Lutheran confession before the assembled emperor, rulers, and churchmen. At the conclusion of his presentation, Chancellor Beyer said to Emperor Charles V, "Most gracious Emperor, this is a Confession which, with the grace and help of God, will prevail even against the gates of hell." That day in Augsburg was truly the birthday of the Lutheran Church.

Using This Study Guide

Each of these study guides on the Lutheran Confessions has thirteen sessions. Following a Law/Gospel focus and a litany for worship, sessions are divided into four easy-to-use sections. These are noted in the Leader Guide by their bold, centered titles appearing within the text.

Focus—Section 1 focuses the participant's attention on the key concept that will be discovered in the session.

Inform—Section 2 explores a portion of the Confessions and questions that help the participant study the text.

Connect—Section 3 helps the participant apply the doctrine to their lives.

Vision—Section 4 provides the participant with practical suggestions for taking the theme of the lesson out of the classroom and into the world. This section also concludes with a hymn for worship and a reading assignment for the following week.

May God bless the study of His truth as we celebrate His grace to us through Jesus, our Lord. By the power of the Holy Spirit, may we focus again on the rich heritage that is ours as the people of God in Christ.

Session 1

Bible-Based Truth

The Augsburg Confession: An Introduction

Law/Gospel Focus

God calls us to believe His truth revealed in the Holy Scriptures. Yet we often listen to the traditions and philosophies of this world; we fail to acknowledge and confess that God's Word is the only source for Christian faith and living. By His death and resurrection, Jesus has atoned for our disobedience to the Word of God. For Jesus' sake, God forgives us and by His Holy Spirit empowers us for faithfulness to His Word.

Opening Worship

Read together the following litany based on Hebrews 13.

Leader: Remember your leaders, those who spoke to you the word of God. Consider the outcome of their way of life, and imitate their faith.

Participants: **Jesus Christ is the same yesterday and today and forever.**

Leader: Do not be led away by diverse and strange teachings, for it is good for the heart to be strengthened by grace.

Participants: **Through Him then let us continually offer up a sacrifice of praise to God, that is, the fruit of lips that acknowledge His name.**

Leader: Obey your leaders and submit to them, for they are keeping watch over your souls, as those who will have to give an account.

Participants: **Let them do this with joy and not with groaning, for that would be of no advantage to you.**

All: **Now may the God of peace who brought again from the dead our Lord Jesus, the great shepherd of the sheep, by the blood of the eternal covenant, equip you with everything good that you may do His will, working in us that which is pleasing in His sight, through Jesus Christ, to whom be glory forever and ever. Amen.**

Sign Here

"Sign this confession." Sometimes we speak of a confession as an acknowledgment of wrongdoings. Yet a confession can also be a positive statement of belief. We confess what we believe about someone or something.

The Christian Church has always had statements of what God's people believe, teach, and confess. Rooted in the sacred Scriptures, these confessions are public statements for all people to read and accept.

1. Statements of belief are common today; clubs and associations often have formal confessions. What kinds of organizations have statements of belief? What do their statements include? Why are these confessions important?

2. Why are Christian Confessions, like the Augsburg Confession, important today?

3. What happens when God's people are not clear about what they believe and confess?

A Complete Summary

The Augsburg Confession

Most invincible Emperor, Caesar Augustus, most clement Lord: Your Imperial Majesty has summoned a meeting of the Empire here at Augsburg. . . . This meeting is also to consider disagreements in our holy religion, the Christian faith, by hearing everyone's opinions and judgments in each other's presence. They are to be considered and evaluated among ourselves in mutual charity, mercy, and kindness. After the removal and correction of things that either side has understood differently, these matters may be settled and brought back to one simple truth and Christian concord. Then we may embrace and maintain the future of one pure and true religion under one Christ. (AC Preface 1–4)

At the very beginning of the meeting in Augsburg, Your Imperial Majesty made a proposal to the electors, princes, and other estates of the Empire. Among other things, you asked that the several estates of the Empire—on the strength of the Imperial edict—should submit their explanations, opinions, and judgments in German and Latin. . . . Therefore, concerning this religious matter, we offer this Confession. It is ours and our preachers'. It shows, from the Holy Scriptures and God's pure Word, what has been up to this time presented in our lands, dukedoms, dominions, and cities, and taught in our churches. (AC Preface 6–8)

There has always been harmonious action and agreement among the electors, princes, and other estates to hold a Council, in all the Imperial Meetings held during Your Majesty's reign. Even before this time, we have appealed this great and grave matter, to the assembly of this General Council, and to your Imperial Majesty, in an appropriate matter. We still stand by this appeal, both to your Imperial Majesty and to a Council. We have no intention to abandon our appeal, with this or any other document. . . .

In regard to this appeal we solemnly and publicly testify here. (AC Preface 21–24)

This then is nearly a complete summary of our teaching. As can be seen, there is nothing that varies from the Scriptures, or from the Church universal, or from the Church of Rome, as known from its writers. Since this is the case, those who insist that our teachers are to be regarded as heretics are judging harshly. There is, however, disagreement on certain abuses that have crept into the Church without rightful authority. Even here, if there are some differences, the bishops should bear with us patiently because of the Confession we have just reviewed. Even the Church's canon law is not so severe that it demands the same rites everywhere. Nor, for that matter, have the rites of all churches ever been the same. (AC XXI, A Summary of the Conflict, 1–3)

Discussing the Text

4. A diet is a parliamentary general assembly of political leaders. Who called the diet at Augsburg? What issue faced the empire? the Church?

5. The primary author of the Augsburg Confession was Philip Melanchthon, friend and co-worker of Martin Luther. In what sense, though, does the Augsburg Confession represent all evangelicals of the time?

6. Describe the tone of the Preface. Why was it important to write and speak this way?

7. What two points did the confessors at Augsburg want to demonstrate with their Confession?

8. In what ways do the confessors take their responsibility seriously?

9. What action did the Lutheran confessors request of Emperor Charles V in the event that the differences between the Lutherans and the Roman Catholics were not peacefully settled?

Defending the Faith

After the Augsburg Confession was read aloud and presented to the emperor, a second document was prepared to answer the criticisms brought against the reformers' theology. Philip Melanchthon wrote this confession too: The Apology (or Defense) of the Augsburg Confession. The Apology is the first and most notable commentary on the Augsburg Confession. Like the Augsburg Confession, it assures us that, even though we often waver in our faith and fail to live according to our Christian confession, God in Christ is the One who rescues us from sin and every evil and time and again sets our feet on the right path of faith and life.

The Apology of the Augsburg Confession

Reader, you now have our Apology. From it you will understand not only what the adversaries said about our Confession (for we have reported in good faith), but also that—contrary to the clear Scripture of the Holy Spirit—they condemned several articles. . .

I [Philip Melanchthon] have written with the greatest moderation possible. If any expression appears too severe, I must say that I am arguing with the theologians and monks who wrote the Confutation, not with the emperor or the princes, whom I hold in due esteem. . . .

Yet I did not discuss all their sophistries, for it would be an endless task. Instead I deal with the chief arguments, so that all nations will have a clear testimony from us that we hold the Gospel of Christ correctly and piously. Disagreement does not delight us, neither are we indifferent to our danger. . . . Yet we cannot abandon truth that is clear and necessary for the Church. . . .

We have the public testimony of many good men, who give thanks to God for this great blessing: our Confession teaches many necessary things better than any of our adversaries' books.

We will commend our cause to Christ, who will someday judge these controversies. We beg Him to look upon the afflicted and scattered churches and to bring them back to godly and continuous harmony. (Ap Preface 9–19)

10. Why did the Lutheran confessors find it necessary to draft a reply defending the Augsburg Confession?

11. Characterize and evaluate Philip Melanchthon's tone in writing the Apology of the Augsburg Confession. What can we learn from him for our sharing the Gospel today? (See also 1 Peter 3:15–16.)

12. What are some of the difficulties and dangers that we can expect as we witness our faith "so that all nations will have a clear testimony from us that we hold the Gospel of Christ correctly and piously"?

13. What does Melanchthon pray for God's Church? What can we, as God's redeemed people in Christ, pray for the Church and her mission today?

Life in the Body

Personal Reflection

- Ask a friend what he or she thinks about the value of confessions of faith in the Church. Share what you believe about the importance of your confession.
- Read Ephesians 4:1–16. How does St. Paul's imagery of the body help you understand the Church and your life in Christ?
- Write a brief confession of a Christian belief dear to you. Share it with God in prayer.

Family Connection

- Read Philippians 2:5–11 as a confession of the servanthood, salvation work, and exaltation of Jesus Christ. Talk about why Jesus Christ became "obedient to the point of death, even death on a cross."
- Pray together for the Christian Church throughout the world. Ask God to restore His Church to "godly and continuous harmony."
- Share what the words of St. Paul to Timothy in 2 Timothy 3:14–17 tell you about the necessity, character, and purposes of Holy Scriptures.

Closing Worship

Sing or pray together "O Word of God Incarnate" (*Lutheran Worship* 335).

O Word of God incarnate,
O Wisdom from on high,
O Truth unchanged, unchanging,
O Light of our dark sky:
We praise You for the radiance
That from the hallowed page,
A lantern to our footsteps,
Shines on from age to age.

The Church from You, dear Master,
Received the gift divine;
And still that light is lifted
O'er all the earth to shine.
It is the chart and compass

That, all life's voyage through,
Mid mists and rocks and quicksands
Still guides, O Christ, to You.

Oh, make Your Church, dear Savior,
A lamp of burnished gold
To bear before the nations
Your true light as of old!
Oh, teach Your wand'ring pilgrims
By this their path to trace
Till, clouds and darkness ended,
They see You face to face!

For Next Week

Read Article I of the Augsburg Confession.

Session 2

God: One Essence, Three Persons

Article I

Law/Gospel Focus

The Bible proclaims the triune God—one divine essence in three persons. God commands all people to fear, love, and trust in Him above all things. Because of our sinful nature, however, we follow our own ideas of God and make our own idols. Yet God graciously forgives our failures to acknowledge Him. In love, the Father sent His Son into the world to pay the debt for our sins. The Holy Spirit works faith in our hearts to trust and worship the one true God.

Opening Worship

Read together the following litany based on Ephesians 1.

Leader: Blessed be the God and Father of our Lord Jesus Christ, who has blessed us in Christ with every spiritual blessing in the heavenly places,

Participants: **even as He chose us in Him before the foundation of the world, that we should be holy and blameless before Him.**

Leader: In love He predestined us for adoption through Jesus Christ, according to the purpose of His will, to the praise of His glorious grace, with which He has blessed us in the Beloved.

Participants: **In Him we have redemption through His blood, the forgiveness of our trespasses, according to the riches of**

15

His grace, which He lavished upon us, in all wisdom and insight

Leader: making known to us the mystery of His will, according to His purpose, which He set forth in Christ as a plan for the fullness of time, to unite all things in Him, things in heaven and things on earth.

Participants: **In Him we have obtained an inheritance, having been predestined according to the purpose of Him who works all things according to the counsel of His will, so that we who were the first to hope in Christ might be to the praise of His glory.**

Designer Gods

Voltaire wrote, "If there were no God, it would be necessary to invent Him." The truth is, however, that human beings could never invent the God who is and who has revealed Himself in Holy Scripture.

The Augsburg Confession, therefore, begins with a statement on who God is, what God is like, and how God relates to the world.

14. Share, as possible, what different religions believe and teach about "God."

15. In what ways today do people design their own gods?

We Uphold Nicaea

The Augsburg Confession

Our churches teach with common consent that the decree of the Council of Nicaea about the unity of the divine essence and the three persons is true. It is to be believed without any doubt. God is one divine essence who is eternal, without a body, without parts, of infinite power, wisdom, and goodness. He is the maker and preserver of all things, visible and invisible (Nehemiah 9:6). Yet there are three persons, the Father, the Son, and the Holy Spirit (Matthew 28:19). These three persons are of the same essence and power. . . .

Our churches condemn all heresies (Titus 3:10–11) that arose against this article, such as the Manichaeans, who assumed that there are two "principles," one Good and the other Evil. They also condemn the Valentinians, Arians, Eunomians, Muslims, and all heresies such as these. (AC I 1–5)

Discussing the Text

16. Why did the confessors begin with a statement on *God?* In what ways did they root Article I in the faith of the historic, *universal* Church?

17. Describe, in your own words, the doctrine of God set forth in Article I.

18. List God's attributes mentioned in Article I.

19. What works of God are highlighted in Article I?

20. Mani and his followers (third century) believed in two equal principles or gods: good and evil. Valentinus and his followers (second century) were Gnostics who denied the incarnation. Arius and his followers (fourth century) believed that Jesus was not truly divine. In

what ways do these heresies deny and contradict the biblical truth about the triune God?

21. Skim Psalm 104. In what ways does the psalmist portray the attributes and works of God?

22. If the confessors wrote today, what false teachings about God would they confront and reject?

God Is Triune

Like the Augsburg Confession, the Apology affirms the truth of the triune God, who alone is worthy of one worship and praise. Yet we remember that we have often failed to fear, love, and trust the true God above all things. Too often we look to things and persons as having the highest importance in our lives rather than God. The triune God is the God of our salvation, forgiving us our sins, calling us to faith and faithfulness, and empowering us to do what we cannot do by ourselves—fear, love, and trust Him above all things. God the Father has sent His Son to be our Savior. By His life, death, and resurrection, the Son has made it possible for us to be restored to God's presence and power. The Holy Spirit gifts us with saving faith in Jesus Christ as Savior and renews our lives to will and do God's good pleasure.

The Apology of the Augsburg Confession

Our adversaries approve Article I of our Confession, in which we declare that we believe and teach that there is one divine, undivided essence. Yet, there are three distinct persons, of the same divine essence, and coeternal: Father, Son, and Holy Spirit.

We have always taught and defended this article. We believe that it has sure and firm testimonies in Holy Scripture that cannot be overthrown. We constantly affirm that those thinking otherwise are outside of Christ's Church, are idolaters, and insult God. (Ap I 1–2)

23. Share how the saving work of the triune God—Father, Son, and Holy Spirit—shapes your daily attitudes and life.

24. Why was it important for Melanchthon to write, "We have always taught and defended this article"?

25. What do the following passages reveal about the triune God?

And when Jesus was baptized, immediately He went up from the water, and behold, the heavens were opened to Him, and He saw the Spirit of God descending like a dove and coming to rest on Him; and behold, a voice from heaven said, "This is My beloved Son, with whom I am well pleased." (Matthew 3:16–17)

The grace of the Lord Jesus Christ and the love of God and the fellowship of the Holy Spirit be with you all. (2 Corinthians 13:14)

26. How do the confessors show their unswerving commitment to the Holy Scriptures?

In the Name

Personal Reflection

- Meditate on these words spoken when water was applied to you in Holy Baptism: "In the name of the Father and of the Son and of the Holy Spirit."
- Use the words of a favorite hymn to praise the Father, the Son, and the Holy Spirit for your salvation.
- The Twelve Step Spiritual Program of Recovery used in a variety of mutual help groups speaks of God as "a Power greater than ourselves" and as "God as we understood Him." Consider how you might be helpful to a family member, friend, or acquaintance who practices the Twelve Steps.

Family Connection

- Read the Nicene Creed together. Discuss how the creed is related to Article I of the Augsburg Confession.
- In the Small Catechism, Dr. Martin Luther suggests, "In the morning, when you rise, you shall bless yourself with the holy cross and say, In the name of God the Father, Son, and Holy Spirit. Amen." Discuss how remembering and speaking these words in the morning and making the sign of the cross will remind you of your Baptism.
- Identify television programs or movies that speak of God without making reference to Father, Son, and Holy Spirit. Why do you think they speak of God as they do? How do such presentations both help and hinder our Christian witness?

Closing Worship

Sing or pray together "Come, O Almighty King" (*LW* 169).

Come, O almighty King,
Help us Your name to sing;
Help us to praise;
Father all-glorious,
In all victorious,
Come and reign over us,
Ancient of Days.

Come, O incarnate Word,
Gird on Your mighty sword;
Our prayer attend.
Come and Your people bless,
And give Your Word success,
And let Your righteousness
On us descend.

Come, holy Comforter,
Your sacred witness bear
In this glad hour!
Your sev'nfold gifts impart;
Rule now in ev'ry heart;
Never from us depart,
Spirit of pow'r.

To the great One in Three
Eternal praises be
Hence evermore!
Your sov'reign majesty
May we in glory see
And to eternity
Love and adore.

For Next Week

Read Articles II, XVIII, and XIX of the Augsburg Confession.

Session 3

Sin and Free Will

Articles II, XVIII, and XIX

Law/Gospel Focus

By nature all human beings are sinful; we daily sin much. We often trust our own abilities in spiritual matters and believe we can do what truly pleases God. The Scriptures remind us, therefore, that apart from God's intervention we are lost and condemned creatures. Yet, while we were still sinners, Christ died for us. For Jesus' sake, God comes to us and makes us spiritually alive. The Holy Spirit calls us to faith and new life in Christ.

Opening Worship

Read together the following litany based on Psalm 51.

Leader: Have mercy on me, O God,

Participants: **according to Your steadfast love; according to Your abundant mercy blot out my transgressions.**

Leader: Wash me thoroughly from my iniquity, and cleanse me from my sin!

Participants: **For I know my transgressions, and my sin is ever before me.**

Leader: Against You, You only, have I sinned and done what is evil in Your sight,

Participants: **so that You may be justified in Your words and blameless in Your judgment.**

Leader: Behold, I was brought forth in iniquity, and in sin did my mother conceive me.

Participants: **Purge me with hyssop, and I shall be clean; wash me, and I shall be whiter than snow.**

Leader: Let me hear joy and gladness; let the bones that You have broken rejoice.

Participants: **Hide Your face from my sins, and blot out all my iniquities.**

All: **Create in me a clean heart, O God, and renew a right spirit within me. Cast me not away from Your presence, and take not Your Holy Spirit from me. Restore to me the joy of Your salvation, and uphold me with a willing spirit.**

Don't Mention It?

A New England primer observed, "In Adam's Fall We sinned all." Yet *sin* is not a popular word in our culture. Many people reject the belief that we are all sinful from birth. Others want to avoid the word *sin* altogether. We may feel comfortable talking about frailty and weakness, but we avoid talking about sin. When people hurt and harm others, they are not seen as sinful people whose actions are sins; their behavior is blamed on bad genes, faulty environment, or a disease like alcoholism.

What is the truth about sin? How does sin impact our lives and our relationship with God? Is there anything we can do to remedy our situation? The Augsburg Confession addresses these questions in three different articles.

27. Why do you think people are reluctant to admit, "I am sinful"?

28. Why are people often reluctant to acknowledge the reality of sin in our world?

29. In what ways do we overestimate our ability to "be" and "do" good?

After the Fall

The Augsburg Confession

Our churches teach that since the fall of Adam (Romans 5:12), all who are naturally born are born with sin (Psalm 51:5), that is, without the fear of God, without trust in God, and with the inclination to sin, called concupiscence. Concupiscence is a disease and original vice that is truly sin. It damns and brings eternal death on those who are not born anew through Baptism and the Holy Spirit (John 3:5).

Our churches condemn the Pelagians and others who deny that original depravity is sin, thus obscuring the glory of Christ's merit and benefits. Pelagians argue that a person can be justified before God by his own strength and reason. (AC II 1–3)

Our churches teach that a person's will has some freedom to choose civil righteousness and to do things subject to reason. It has no power, without the Holy Spirit, to work the righteousness of God, that is, spiritual righteousness. For "the natural person does not accept the things of the Spirit of God" (1 Corinthians 2:14). This righteousness is worked in the heart when the Holy Spirit is received through the Word (Galatians 3:2–6). (AC XVIII 1–3)

Our churches teach that although God creates and preserves nature, the cause of sin is located in the will of the wicked, that is, the devil and ungodly people. Without God's help, this will turns itself away from God, as Christ says, "When he lies, he speaks out of his own character" (John 8:44). (AC XIX)

Discussing the Text

30. What words would you use to describe sin? to describe sin's power and result?

31. Describe the human condition on the basis of Article II.

32. How does hereditary (or original) sin express itself in human life? What does inherited sin make people incapable of doing?

33. What is God's attitude toward sin and sinfulness?

34. The confessors compare original sin to a disease. In what ways is sin like a disease?

35. How does original sin underscore the necessity for the Baptism of children?

36. In what ways is the human will *free?* In what ways is our will absolutely *enslaved?*

37. How does Article XIX describe the cause of sin?

38. Explain your understanding of the words "Without God's help, this will turns itself away from God."

Dead As . . .

A stone. A log. A corpse. The reality is that each of these things is inanimate. A stone cannot move itself. A log cannot attach itself to a living tree. On its own, a corpse cannot live again.

The Apology of the Augsburg Confession elaborates on the truth that we are, by nature, *unable* to fear and love God. Every person is born in sin, as David confesses in Psalm 51. Every person is born dead in transgressions and sins, as St. Paul acknowledges in his letter to the Ephesians (2:1). But God, in His love and mercy, has overcome our sin and death through the gift of forgiveness and life in Christ.

The Apology of the Augsburg Confession

> For what else is being able, by one's own strength, to love God above all things and fulfill His commandments except original righteousness? If human nature is so strong that it is able, on its own, to love God above all things . . . what then is original sin? Why do we need Christ's grace if we can be justified as a result of our own righteousness? Why do we need the Holy Spirit if we are strong enough on our own to love God above all things and fulfill God's commandments? . . . Scripture everywhere warns us, as the Prophets constantly complain, about putting our confidence in our human abilities, contempt for God, hating God, and similar faults with which we are born. (Ap II 9–11)

> We have not said anything new. The ancient definition of original sin, understood correctly, says precisely the same thing. "Original sin is the absence of original righteousness." But what is righ teousness? . . . In the Scriptures, righteousness consists not only

in obeying the Second Table of the Ten Commandments (which are about good works in serving our fellowman), but also the First Table, which teaches about fearing God, faith, and loving God. Therefore, original righteousness includes not only physical health in all ways, as they contend (such as pure blood and unimpaired physical ability), but also these gifts: a sure and certain knowledge of God, fear of God, confidence in God, and the desire and ability to give God these things. Scripture testifies this when it says in Genesis 1:27 that man was made in the image and likeness of God. What else was this image and likeness other than that man was created with wisdom and righteousness so that he could apprehend God and reflect God? Mankind was given the gift of knowing God, fearing God, and being confident in God. (Ap II 15–18)

We are right in our description of original sin when we say that it is not being able to believe God and not being able to fear and love God. We are right when we say that it includes concupiscence, which seeks fleshly things contrary to God's Word. This means when it seeks not only the pleasure of the body, but also fleshly wisdom and righteousness. (Ap II 26)

Since Christ was given to us to remove both these sins and these punishments and to destroy the devil's kingdom, sin, and death (1 John 3:8), we will never be able to recognize Christ's benefits unless we understand our evils. (Ap II 50)

We do not deny freedom to the human will. The human will has freedom in the choice of works and things that reason understands by itself. To a certain extent reason can display public righteousness or the righteousness of works. It can speak of God, offer to God a certain service by an outward work, and obey public officials and parents. In choosing an outward work, it can hold back the hand from murder, adultery, and theft. Because human nature has been left with reason and judgment about objects subjected to the senses, choice between these things, the liberty and power to produce public righteousness, are also left. Scripture calls this the righteousness of the flesh, which the carnal nature (that is, reason) produces by itself, without the Holy Spirit. However, the power of lustful desire is such that people more often obey evil inclinations than sound judgment. The devil, who is powerful in the godless, does not cease to stir up this weak nature to various offenses, as Paul says in Ephesians 2:2. (Ap XVIII 70–71)

Although we admit that free will has the freedom and power to perform the extreme works of the Law, we do not assign spiritual matters to free will. These are to truly fear God, believe God, be confident and hold that He cares for us, hears us, and forgives us. These are the true works of the First Table, which the heart cannot produce without the Holy Spirit, as Paul says, "The natural person [namely, a person using only natural strength] does not accept the things of the Spirit of God" (1 Corinthians 2:14). People can determine this if they consider what their hearts believe about God's will, whether they are truly confident God cares for and hears them. Even the saints find keeping this faith difficult (which is not possible in unbelievers). But, as we have said before, it begins when terrified hearts hear the Gospel and receive comfort.

Their distinction is helpful. Civil righteousness is assigned to free will, and spiritual righteousness is assigned to the governing of the Holy Spirit in the reborn. In this way, outward discipline is kept, because all people should know that God requires this civil righteousness and that, to some extent, we can achieve it. And yet a distinction is shown between human and spiritual righteousness, between philosophical teaching and the teaching of the Holy Spirit. It can be understood why the Holy Spirit is needed. (Ap XVIII 73–75)

39. What two features of original sin do the confessors note in Article II? Share how Christ and Baptism into His death and resurrection change both in your life.

40. How does your faith in Christ strengthen you in times of guilt and temptation?

41. "We will never be able to recognize Christ's benefits unless we understand our evils" (Ap II 50). In what ways are both Law and Gospel vital for God's people?

42. In what ways does the article on free will help you understand human behavior? How does this reality underscore the urgency of Christian witness?

43. Describe the joy of salvation—from beginning to end—in Christ.

To Our Rescue

Personal Reflection

- Remembering God's forgiving love for you in Christ, confess your sins that you may know the magnitude of the grace of Christ.
- Read Romans 7:14–25. How do these words of St. Paul express your own life experience as a Christian? How does Jesus minister to you as your deliverer?
- During the week as you come into contact with non-Christians, note how they exercise their ability to achieve civil righteousness to do good things for the benefit of others.
- Notice from your social contacts, TV, newspapers, and magazines how people obey their evil impulses more often than their sound judgment.

Family Connection

- Thank God for the good that non-Christians do for the benefit of your community and nation. Pray that they may become spiritually

and eternally alive through faith in Jesus Christ and, renewed by the
Holy Spirit, may honor God and serve others in ways that truly
please Him.

- Share together the blessings of your Baptism into Christ.
- Read together the Third Article of the Apostles' Creed and Luther's explanation in the Catechism. How do the words reflect
  what Scripture and the Augsburg Confession teach about original
  sin and freedom of the will?

Closing Worship

Sing or pray together "Chief of Sinners Though I Be" (*LW* 285).

Chief of sinners though I be,
Jesus shed His blood for me,
Died that I might live on high,
Lives that I might never die.
As the branch is to the vine,
I am His, and He is mine.

Oh, the height of Jesus' love,
Higher than the heav'ns above,
Deeper than the depths of sea,
Lasting as eternity!
Love that found me—wondrous thought—
Found me when I sought Him not.

O my Savior, help afford
By Your Spirit and Your Word!
When my wayward heart would stray,
Keep me in the narrow way;
Grace in time of need supply
While I live and when I die.

For Next Week

Read Articles III and XXI of the Augsburg Confession.

Session 4

Jesus Christ: God's Son, Savior, and Intercessor

Articles III and XXI

Law/Gospel Focus

Because of our sinful nature and desires, we often fail to recognize Jesus as our Lord and Savior. We make other saviors in our own image. We rely on ourselves and live in self-serving ways. Yet the Son of God came down from heaven for us and for our salvation. Jesus forgives us and all His repentant people and empowers us boldly to confess Him as the Son of God made flesh, our only Savior and intercessor with the Father.

Opening Worship

Read together the following litany based on John 1.

Leader: In the beginning was the Word, and the Word was with God, and the Word was God. He was in the beginning with God.

Participants: **All things were made through Him, and without Him was not anything made that was made.**

Leader: In Him was life, and the life was the light of men. The light shines in the darkness, and the darkness has not overcome it.

Participants: **And the Word became flesh and dwelt among us, and we have seen His glory, glory as of the only Son from the Father, full of grace and truth.**

Leader: And from His fullness we have all received, grace upon grace. For the law was given through Moses; grace and truth came through Jesus Christ.

Participants: **No one has ever seen God; the only God, who is at the Father's side, He has made Him known.**

More Than a Fish Story

In the Early Church the simple outline of a fish became a Christian confession and identification sign. In Greek the five letters of the word *fish*—IChThUS—helped believers to remember the truth of the Gospel: *Iesous* (Jesus) *Christos* (Christ) *Theou* (God's) *Uios* (Son) *Soter* (Savior).

"Jesus Christ is the Son of God and Savior." This confession is the Church's one foundation. The Augsburg Confession presents the simple truths of Holy Scripture on the person and work of Jesus Christ.

44. How has our world's understanding of Jesus changed in the past years?

45. What ideas about Jesus do you hear in your conversations with others? What ideas have you noticed in the media?

God and Man

The Augsburg Confession

Our churches teach that the Word, that is, the Son of God (John 1:14), assumed the human nature in the womb of the Blessed Virgin Mary. So there are two natures—the divine and the human—inseparably joined in one person. There is one Christ, true God and true man, who was born of the Virgin Mary, truly suffered, was crucified, died, and was buried. He did this to reconcile the Father to us and to be a sacrifice, not only for original guilt, but also for all actual sins of mankind (John 1:29).

He also descended into hell, and truly rose again on the third day. Afterward, He ascended into heaven to sit at the right hand of the Father. There He forever reigns and has dominion over all creatures. He sanctifies those who believe in Him, by sending the Holy Spirit into their hearts to rule, comfort, and make them alive. He defends them against the devil and the power of sin.

The same Christ will openly come again to judge the living and the dead, and so forth, according to the Apostles' Creed. (AC III)

Our churches teach that the history of saints may be set before us so that we may follow the example of their faith and good works, according to our calling. . . .

But the Scriptures do not teach that we are to call on the saints or to ask the saints for help. Scripture sets before us the one Christ as the Mediator, Atoning Sacrifice, High Priest, and Intercessor (1 Timothy 2:5–6). He is to be prayed to. He has promised that He will hear our prayer (John 14:13). This is the worship that He approves above all other worship, that He be called upon in all afflictions. "If anyone does sin, we have an advocate with the Father" (1 John 2:1). (AC XXI)

Discussing the Text

46. Jesus is the true God. What words describe His deity? How did He show His divine nature and power on earth?

47. Jesus is true man. What words describe His humanity? How did He show His human nature on earth?

48. Why is it necessary for Christ to be both God and man?

49. What major events of the God-man's life and ministry are noted in Article III? What other events do you recall from the four Gospels? Relate the events to the Church year.

50. Why, according to Article III, did Christ die?

51. Since His ascension, what does Christ do for His redeemed people?

52. Why, do you suppose, did the confessors rely on the Apostles' Creed for the article on Christ?

53. In what ways is it helpful for God's people to remember the saints? What abuses can result?

54. High Priest. Advocate. Intercessor. What do these titles reveal about Jesus and His Gospel?

As a God

Early in the second century, the Roman governor Pliny wrote to Emperor Trajan, "[Christians] usually come together before daybreak and sing hymns back and forth to Christ as a god." Pliny was closer to the truth than he knew. But Christ is not godlike: He is true God who became a human being. He is the God-man who paid the debt for our sins. We sing hymns to Him and pray to Him, for He is our intercessor before the Father.

The Apology of the Augsburg Confession

We confess that there are two natures in Christ. The human nature is assumed by the Word into the unity of His person (John 1:14). Christ suffered and died to reconcile the Father to us and was raised again to reign, to justify, and to sanctify believers according to the Apostles' Creed and the Nicene Creed. (Ap III)

Our Confession approves honoring the saints in three ways. The first is thanksgiving. We should thank God because He has shown examples of mercy, because He wishes to save people, and because He has given teachers and other gifts to the Church. . . . The second service is the strengthening of our faith. When we see Peter's denial forgiven, we also are encouraged to believe all the more that grace truly superabounds over sin (Romans 5:20). The third honor is the imitation, first of faith, then of the other virtues. Everyone should imitate the saints according to his calling. . . .

Our Confession affirms only this: Scripture does not teach the invocation of the saints, or that we are to ask the saints for aid. Since neither a command nor a promise nor an example can be produced from the Scriptures about the invocation of saints, it makes sense that conscience remains uncertain about this invocation. Since prayer should be made from faith, how do we know that God approves this invocation? Without the testimony of Scripture, how do we know that the saints know about the prayers of each one? . . .

The second requirement for an atonement maker is that his merits are shown to make satisfaction for other people. They are divinely given to others, so that through them, just as by their own merits, other people may be regarded righteous. For example, when any friend pays a debt for a friend, the debtor is freed by the merit of another, as though it were by his own. So Christ's merits are given to us so that, when we believe in Him, we may be regarded righteous by our confidence in Christ's merits as though we had merits of our own.

From both of these—the promise and the giving of merits—arises confidence in mercy. Such confidence in the divine promise, and likewise in Christ's merits, should be promoted when we pray. For we should be truly confident, both that for Christ's sake we are heard and that by His merits we have a reconciled Father. (Ap XXI 4–20)

55. Share, in your own words, who Christ is and what He has done for you. What new insight into His saving work do you have today?

56. How do the Apostles' and Nicene Creeds underlie and promote Article III? What does the Nicene Creed confess that is especially relevant to Christ?

57. What does it mean to you that Jesus is your *divine and human* Savior?

58. In what ways can you honor the saints of the past in your life?

59. Describe your comfort in knowing Jesus as the propitiation for your sin and your only intercessor.

As an Example

Personal Reflection

- Pray to God the Father, in the name of Jesus, for some special gift you would like to receive and use to Christ's glory.
- Think of two or three saints for whom you have great respect. How can you draw strength from the example of God's grace in their lives?
- Consider whether or not, from time to time, you have attitudes that devalue the merits of Jesus Christ in your life. Confess such faults and ask God for forgiveness and a life that gives Jesus His proper place.
- Read John 17 to discover how Jesus, shortly before His death, carried out His role as intercessor. What comfort and strength do you find for your life in His words?

Family Connection

- During the week, take note of how people disparage the person and work of Jesus Christ. Pray that they may come to a right understanding of Jesus and trust in Him as the God-man who came from heaven for us and our salvation.
- Confess your faith together in the Second Article of the Apostles' Creed and Luther's explanation. Identify the past, present, and future events in the life of Jesus Christ.
- Ask each family member to share his or her confirmation verse. Relate the truth of the verse to the person and work of Jesus Christ.

Closing Worship

Sing or pray together "Glory Be to God the Father" (*LW* 173).

Glory be to God the Father,
Glory be to God the Son,
Glory be to God the Spirit:
Great Jehovah, Three in One!
Glory, glory
While eternal ages run!

Glory be to Him who loved us,
Washed us from each spot and stain;

Glory be to Him who bought us,
Made us kings with Him to reign!
Glory, glory
To the Lamb that once was slain!

Glory, blessing, praise eternal!
Thus the choir of angels sings;
Honor, riches, pow'r, dominion!
Thus its praise creation brings.
Glory, glory,
Glory to the King of kings!

For Next Week

Read the selections from Article IV of the Augsburg Confession and its Apology.

Session 5

Justification: Righteousness before God

Article IV

Law/Gospel Focus

Though reason can produce civic righteousness—outward works based on our natural knowledge of God's Law—our efforts cannot obtain for us forgiveness of sin and righteousness before God. We are lost and condemned creatures apart from God. Yet God has planned from eternity for us to receive forgiveness of sin and be righteous in His sight. In Christ, our heavenly Father justifies us, calls us to faith, renews our hope, and equips us to serve Him daily.

Opening Worship

Read together the following litany based on Psalm 32:1–7.

Leader: Blessed is the one whose transgression is forgiven, whose sin is covered.

Participants: **Blessed is the man against whom the LORD counts no iniquity, and in whose spirit there is no deceit.**

Leader: For when I kept silent, my bones wasted away through my groaning all day long.

Participants: **For day and night Your hand was heavy upon me; my strength was dried up as by the heat of summer.**

Leader: I acknowledged my sin to You, and I did not cover up my iniquity;

Participants: **I said, "I will confess my transgressions to the LORD," and You forgave the inquity of my sin.**

Leader: Therefore let everyone who is godly offer prayer to You at a time when You may be found; surely in the rush of great waters, they shall not reach him.

Participants: **You are a hiding place for me; You preserve me from trouble; You surround me with shouts of deliverance.**

Straight to the Heart

"My country is the world," wrote Thomas Paine in *The Rights of Man*, "and my religion is to do good." In a few simple words the American revolutionary described the heart and center of his "faith."

What is the heart and center of the Christian faith? Why is it central and chief? The Augsburg Confession clearly presents the central teaching of Christianity in Article IV.

60. What understandings of the Christian faith do people express today?

61. How would you explain the Christian faith to an inquiring person?

Faith as Righteousness

The Augsburg Confession

Our churches teach that people cannot be justified before God by their own strength, merits, or works. People are freely justified for Christ's sake, through faith, when they believe that they are received into favor and that their sins are forgiven for Christ's sake. By His death, Christ made satisfaction for our sins. God counts this faith for righteousness in His sight (Romans 3:21–26; 4:5). (AC IV)

The Apology of the Augsburg Confession

In this controversy, the chief topic of Christian doctrine is treated. When it is understood correctly, it illumines and amplifies Christ's honor. It brings necessary and most abundant consolation to devout consciences. . . .

All Scripture ought to be distributed into these two principal topics: the Law and the promises. For in some places Scripture presents the Law, and in others the promises about Christ. In other words, in the Old Testament, Scripture promises that Christ will come, and it offers, for His sake, the forgiveness of sins, justification, and life eternal. Or in the Gospel, in the New Testament, Christ Himself (since He has appeared) promises the forgiveness of sins, justification, and life eternal. Furthermore, in this discussion, by *Law* we mean the Ten Commandments, wherever they are read in the Scriptures. (Ap IV 2–6)

We think about the righteousness of reason like this: God requires it. Because of God's commandment, the honorable works commanded by the Ten Commandments must be done. . . . We cheerfully credit this righteousness of reason with the praises that are due it. . . . God also honors it with bodily rewards. However, it ought not to be praised by dishonoring Christ.

So it is false that we merit forgiveness of sins by our works.

It is false that people are counted righteous before God because of the righteousness of reason.

It is false that reason, by its own strength, is able to love God above all things and to fulfill God's Law. In other words, reason cannot truly fear God, be truly confident that God hears prayer, be willing to obey God in death and other divine matters, not covet what belongs to others, and so on. Yet reason can do civil works. (Ap IV 22–27)

By their own strength, people cannot fulfill God's Law. They are all under sin, subject to eternal wrath and death. Because of this, we cannot be freed by the Law from sin and be justified. But the promise of forgiveness of sins and of justification has been given us for Christ's sake, who was given for us in order that He might make satisfaction for the sins of the world. He has been appointed as the Mediator and Atoning Sacrifice. This promise does not depend on our merits, but freely offers forgiveness of sins and justification, as Paul says in Romans 11:6, "But if it is by grace, it is no longer on the basis of works; otherwise grace would no longer be grace." And in another place, Romans 3:21, "The righteousness of God has been manifested apart from the law." In other words, forgiveness of sins is freely offered. Nor does reconciliation depend on our merits. Because if forgiveness of sins were to depend on our merits, and reconciliation were from the Law, it would be useless. Since we do not fulfill the Law, it would also follow that we would never gain the promise of reconciliation. . . .

Since justification is gained through the free promise, it follows that we cannot justify ourselves. Otherwise, why would there be a need to promise? Since the promise can only be received by faith, the Gospel (which is properly the promise of forgiveness of sins and of justification for Christ's sake) proclaims the righteousness of faith in Christ. The Law does not teach this, nor is this the righteousness of the Law. For the Law demands our works and our perfection. But, for Christ's sake, the Gospel freely offers reconciliation to us, who have been vanquished by sin and death. This is received not by works, but by faith alone. This faith does not bring to God confidence in one's own merits, but only confidence in the promise, or the mercy promised in Christ. This special faith (by which an individual believes that for Christ's sake his sins are forgiven him, and that for Christ's sake God is reconciled and sees us favorably) gains forgiveness of sins and justifies us. (Ap IV 40–45)

Discussing the Text

62. In what ways is it "natural" to believe that we are justified by what we do?

63. Summarize, in your own words, how we obtain forgiveness of sin and righteousness before God.

64. What does it mean that we receive *forgiveness of sin from God?* that we receive *righteousness before* God?

65. Why is being "freely justified for Christ's sake, through faith" the "chief topic of Christian doctrine"? (AC IV 2; Ap IV 2)

66. Skim Romans 4. In what ways does Abraham illustrate justification through faith?

67. From the Apology, describe God's grace.

68. Give examples of Scripture passages that reveal and proclaim God's Law.

69. Give examples of Scripture passages that reveal and proclaim God's Gospel.

The Main Doctrine

The Apology goes to great lengths—in the longest article of all!—to defend "the chief topic of Christian doctrine." Our faith must, the confessors agreed, rest on this pillar: that God, in His grace, declares us just—righteous—before Him when we believe that Jesus died for our forgiveness and rose for our eternal salvation. Without this truth, the Church would simply be another "religion." With this Gospel, however, the Church—God's Church—brings light and life to the world.

The Apology of the Augsburg Confession

The promise should always be in sight. Because of His promise, God wishes to be gracious and to justify for Christ's sake, not because of the Law or our works. In this promise timid consciences should seek reconciliation and justification. By this promise they should sustain themselves and be confident that they have a gracious God for Christ's sake, because of His promise. So works can never make a conscience peaceful. Only the promise can. If justification and peace of conscience must be sought in something other than love and works, then love and works do not justify. This is true even though they are virtues and belong to the righteousness of the Law, insofar as they are a fulfilling of the Law. . . .

From this it is clear that *we are justified before God through faith alone*. Through faith alone we receive forgiveness of sins and reconciliation, because reconciliation or justification is a matter promised for Christ's sake, not for the Law's sake. Therefore, it is received through faith alone, although, when the Holy Spirit is given, the fulfilling of the Law follows. (Ap V 59–61; or Ap IV 180–82 in some versions)

70. "God wishes to be gracious and to justify for Christ's sake." In what ways does God show His mercy and goodness in Christ to you?

71. Describe a time when you were plagued in your conscience. How does God's Word bring you assurance amid doubt and temptation?

72. In what ways are our love and works in Christ an outflowing of the Gospel?

73. Characterize the faith by which we obtain the forgiveness of sins and are justified before God.

To God Alone

Personal Reflection

- Meditate on the phrases *grace alone, faith alone,* and *Christ alone.* Thank and praise God for what each of these means for your life.
- As you read newspapers and magazines, watch TV, and surf the Internet, be on the lookout for examples of the "righteousness of the Law."
- Read St. Paul's letter to the Galatians. Make a list of what you learn from Paul about justification by grace through faith.

Family Connection

- Take turns reading Romans 3:21–28. Discuss how we get right with God and how a right relationship with God is possible for us, who by nature are sinful and unclean and separated from God.

- Make a banner or mobile on the doctrine of justification. Be sure to use the words *justified, by grace, through faith,* and *for Christ's sake.*
- Listen for Law and Gospel in hymns and contemporary Christian music.

Closing Worship

Sing or pray together "Salvation unto Us Has Come" (*LW* 355).

Salvation unto us has come
    By God's free grace and favor;
Good works cannot avert our doom,
    They help and save us never.
Faith looks to Jesus Christ alone,
Who did for all the world atone;
    He is our one redeemer.

Faith clings to Jesus' cross alone
    And rests in Him unceasing;
And by its fruits true faith is known,
    With love and hope increasing.
For faith alone can justify;
Works serve our neighbor and supply
    The proof that faith is living.

All blessing, honor, thanks, and praise
    To Father, Son, and Spirit,
The God who saved us by His grace;
    All glory to His merit.
O triune God in heav'n above,
You have revealed Your saving love;
    Your blessed name we hallow.

For Next Week

Read the selections from Articles V, XIV, and XXVIII of the Augsburg Confession.

Session 6

The Gospel and the Sacraments

Articles V, XIV, and XXVIII

Law/Gospel Focus

By nature, all people reject God's means of grace. Even God's people fail to honor and support the ministry of the Gospel. Yet God forgives our sins of indifference toward the Good News through the saving work of Jesus Christ. His forgiveness presents us righteous before our Father and gives us a greater devotion to the ministry of Word and Sacraments.

Opening Worship

Read together the following litany based on Romans 1.

Leader: Paul, a servant of Christ Jesus, called to be an apostle, set apart for the gospel of God,

Participants: **which He promised beforehand through His prophets in the holy Scriptures, concerning His Son,**

Leader: who was descended from David according to the flesh

Participants: **and was declared to be the Son of God in power according to the Spirit of holiness by His resurrection from the dead, Jesus Christ our Lord,**

Leader: through whom we have received grace and apostleship to bring about the obedience of faith for the sake of His name among all the nations,

Participants: **including you who are called to belong to Jesus Christ.**

Leader: For I am not ashamed of the gospel, for it is the power of God for salvation to everyone who believes, to the Jew first and also to the Greek.

Participants: **For in it the righteousness of God is revealed from faith for faith, as it is written, "The righteous shall live by faith."**

A Miraculous Gift

"Faith," wrote Walter Lowrie, "is the gift of God, it is a 'miracle.'" God's forgiveness is a gift that He gives freely and willingly. But His gift is of no value unless we possess it, that is, receive it.

God wants His people to believe—to trust His promises. So He gives another gift: faith itself. We cannot by our reason or strength obtain faith. God, in His goodness, tells us how we obtain His gift. This is the subject of Article V.

74. How do people understand faith?

75. What are some common perceptions about ministers and their work?

Means of the Means

The Augsburg Confession

So that we may obtain this faith, the ministry of teaching the Gospel and administering the Sacraments was instituted. Through the Word and Sacraments, as through instruments, the Holy Spirit is given (John 20:22). He works faith, when and where it pleases God (John 3:8), in those who hear the good news that God justifies those who believe that they are received into grace for Christ's sake. This happens not through our own merits, but for Christ's sake. (AC V 1–3)

Our churches teach that no one should publicly teach in the Church, or administer the Sacraments, without a rightly ordered call. (AC XIV)

Our teachers' position is this: the authority of the Keys (Matthew 16:19), or the authority of the bishops—according to the Gospel—is a power or commandment of God, to preach the Gospel, to forgive and retain sins, and to administer Sacraments. Christ sends out His apostles with this command, "As the Father has sent Me, even so I am sending you . . . Receive the Holy Spirit. If you forgive the sins of anyone, they are forgiven; if you withhold forgiveness from anyone, it is withheld" (John 20:21–22). And in Mark 16:15, Christ says, "Go . . . proclaim the Gospel to the whole creation."

This authority is exercised only by teaching or preaching the Gospel and administering the Sacraments, either to many or to individuals, according to their calling. In this way are given not only bodily, but also eternal things: eternal righteousness, the Holy Spirit, and eternal life. These things cannot reach us except by the ministry of the Word and the Sacraments, as Paul says, "The Gospel . . . is the power of God for salvation to everyone that believes" (Romans 1:16). Therefore, the Church has the authority to grant eternal things and exercises this authority only by the ministry of the Word. So it does not interfere with civil government. (AC XXVIII 5–10)

Again, the only authority that belongs to the bishops is what they have according to the Gospel, or by divine right, as they say. For they have been given the ministry of the Word and Sacraments. They have no other authority according to the Gospel than the authority to forgive sins, to judge doctrine, to reject doctrines contrary to the Gospel, and to exclude from the communion of the Church wicked people, whose wickedness is known. They cannot exclude people with human force, but simply by the Word. (AC XXVIII 21)

Discussing the Text

76. What does Article V presuppose about our human condition? about God's will and purpose for humankind?

77. What are the means of grace? What does God give and produce through His chosen means?

78. Describe the relationship between the means of grace and the Office of the Ministry.

79. In light of Jesus' words to Nicodemus in John 3:5–8, explain the phrase "the Holy Spirit . . . who works faith, when and where it pleases God" (AC V 2; see also John 3:8).

80. Summarize, in your own words, Article XIV.

81. According to Article XIV, how do certain individuals enter the Office of the Ministry? In what way is their office a *public* office?

82. As ministers of the Gospel do their work, what gifts are imparted to people?

83. Describe how ministers of the Gospel continue the work of Christ.

84. What distinctions do the confessors make between Church authority and secular, government authority?

All Gift

The forgiveness of sins is God's gift. Faith that obtains forgiveness is God's gift. In God's plan for bestowing forgiveness, ministers of the Gospel also are splendid gifts (Ephesians 4:10–15). They serve God and administer His means of grace to people in the name and stead of Christ. By His goodness, God restores us sinful people to His presence and power.

The Apology of the Augsburg Confession

In this matter our consciences are not in danger. Since we know that our Confession is true, godly, and catholic, we should not approve the cruelty of those who persecute this doctrine. We know that the Church is among those who teach God's Word rightly and administer the Sacraments rightly. The Church it is not with those who try hard to wipe out God's Word by their orders and also put to death those who teach what is right and true. Toward them even the very canons are gentler, even though they do something contrary to the canons. Furthermore, we want to declare again that we will gladly keep Church and canonical government, so long as the bishops stop attacking our churches. Our request will acquit us, both before God and among all nations forever, from the charge that we have undermined the authority of the bishops. (Ap XIV 26–28)

We must keep in the Church the doctrine that we receive the forgiveness of sins freely for Christ's sake, through faith. We must also keep the doctrine that human traditions are useless services and, therefore, neither sin nor righteousness should be placed in meat, drink, clothing, and like things. Christ wished the use of such things to be left free, since He says, "It is not what goes into the mouth that defiles a person" (Matthew 15:11); and Paul says, "The kingdom of God is not a matter of eating and drinking" (Romans 14:17). Therefore, the bishops have no right to enact traditions in addition to the Gospel, so that people must merit the forgiveness of sins, or that they think are services that God approves as righteousness. They must not burden consciences (as though it were a sin to leave such observances undone). All this is taught by that one passage in Acts 15:9, where the apostles (Peter) say that hearts are cleansed through faith. Then they prohibit the imposing of a yoke and show how great a danger this is, and multiply the sin of those who burden the Church. "Why do you tempt God?" they say. (Ap XXVIII 7–8)

We have declared in the Confession what kind of power the Gospel assigns to bishops. . . . Therefore, the bishop has the power of the order, that is, the ministry of the Word and Sacraments. He also has the power of jurisdiction. This means the authority to excommunicate those guilty of open crimes and again to absolve them if they are converted and seek absolution (John 20:23). But their power is not to be tyrannical, without a fixed law. Nor is it to be regal, above the law.

Rather, they have a fixed command and a fixed Word of God, according to which they should teach and exercise their jurisdiction. Even though they should have some temporal jurisdiction, it does not mean that they are able to set up new services. Spiritual services have nothing to do with temporal jurisdiction. They have the Word, the command, and how far they should exercise jurisdiction, if anyone did anything contrary to that Word they have received from Christ.

In the Confession we also have discussed to what extent they may legitimately enact traditions, not as necessary services, but only for the sake of order in the Church and for peace. These traditions should not entrap consciences, as though to require necessary services. Paul teaches when he says, "Stand firm therefore, and do not submit again to a yoke of slavery" (Galatians 5:1). The use of such ordinances should be left free, so long as offenses are avoided and they are not determined to be necessary services. (Ap XXVIII 12–16)

85. Share the importance of the Gospel and the Sacraments in your life and the life of your congregation.

86. In what ways do God's people show disregard for the Gospel and the Sacraments?

87. In what ways has pastoral ministry changed since the confessors' day? In what ways has it remained the same?

88. How can you and your congregation support your pastor(s) and the Office of the Public Ministry?

Giving Thanks

Personal Reflection

- In your personal conversations, practice different ways of saying the Gospel.
- Recall what the Holy Spirit has done—and still does— for you through the Gospel. Speak a prayer to the Holy Spirit, expressing thanks for each of His benefits in your life.
- Speak a prayer for your pastor, thanking God for his Gospel ministry and asking God to prosper his life and ministry.

Family Connection

- Share with one another a time when the Gospel gave you great comfort and hope.

- Look into ways that you can encourage individuals to consider full-time ministry in the Church.
- Write a note expressing gratitude to your pastor for his ministry. After each member of the family signs the card, put it in the mail with a prayer for God's blessing on his life, family, and service to Christ.

Closing Worship

Sing or pray together "Lord of the Living Harvest" (*LW* 260).

Lord of the living harvest
That whitens on the plain,
Where angels soon shall gather
Their sheaves of golden grain,
Accept these hands to labor,
These hearts to trust and love,
And with them ever hasten
Your kingdom from above.

As lab'rers in Your vineyard,
Help them be ever true,
Content to bear the burden
Of weary days for You,
To ask no other wages
When You will call them home
Than to have shared the labor
That makes Your kingdom come.

Be with them, God the Father,
Be with them, God the Son
And God the Holy Spirit,
Most blessed Three in One.
Teach them, as faithful servants
You rightly to adore,
And fill them with Your fullness
Both now and evermore.

For Next Week

Read the selections from Articles VI and XX of the Augsburg Confession.

Session 7

The New Obedience: Faith and Good Works

Articles VI and XX

Law/Gospel Focus

God's loving gift of justifying faith has the power to bring forth good works in the life of the believer. God does not leave us to live in sin and misery. The Holy Spirit who works faith also produces good works in those who obtain forgiveness of sins and righteousness before God through faith in Jesus Christ. The Spirit enables us to will and to do what God desires for His redeemed people.

Opening Worship

Read together the following litany based on Ephesians 2.

Leader: And you were dead in the trespasses and sins in which you once walked, following the course of this world, following the prince of the power of the air, the spirit that is now at work in the sons of disobedience—

Participants: **among whom we all once lived in the passions of our flesh, carrying out the desires of the body and mind,**

Leader: and were by nature children of wrath, like the rest of mankind.

Participants: **But God, being rich in mercy, because of the great love with which He loved us, even when we were dead in our trespasses, made us alive together with Christ—by grace you have been saved—**

Leader: and raised us up with Him and seated us with Him in the heavenly places in Christ Jesus, so that in the coming ages He might show the immeasurable riches of His grace in kindness toward us in Christ Jesus.

Participants: **For by grace you have been saved through faith. And this is not your own doing; it is the gift of God, not a result of works, so that no one may boast.**

All: **For we are His workmanship, created in Christ Jesus for good works, which God prepared beforehand, that we should walk in them.**

Do All You Can

A tombstone inscription in Shrewsbury, England, reads: "For the Lord Jesus' sake, Do all the good you can, To all the people you can, In all the ways you can."

Do God's people care about doing good works? Does forgiveness of sins and righteousness before God by faith alone—and not by works—mean that we can ignore serving God and others? In Articles VI and XX, the confessors demonstrate that Christians care a great deal about doing works that please God and benefit people.

89. What works do people usually view as good?

90. How do people often look at good works in their lives?

91. What deeds do some people think are better than others?

The Fruit of Faith

The Augsburg Confession

Our churches teach that this faith is bound to bring forth good fruit (Galatians 5:22–23). It is necessary to do good works commanded by God (Ephesians 2:10), because of God's will. We should not rely on those works to merit justification before God. The forgiveness of sins and justification is received through faith. The voice of Christ testifies, "So you also, when you have done all that you were commanded, say, 'We are unworthy servants; we have only done what was our duty'" (Luke 17:10). (AC VI 1–2)

The doctrine about faith, which ought to be the chief doctrine in the Church, has remained unknown for so long. Everyone has to admit that there was the deepest silence in their sermons concerning the righteousness of faith. They only taught about works in the churches. This is why our teachers teach the churches about faith in this way.

First, they teach that our works cannot reconcile God to us or merit forgiveness of sins, grace, and justification. We obtain reconciliation only by faith when we believe that we are received into favor for Christ's sake. He alone has been set forth as the Mediator and Atoning Sacrifice (1 Timothy 2:5), in order that the Father may be reconciled through Him. Therefore, whoever believes that he merits grace by works despises the merit and grace of Christ (Galatians 5:4). (Ap XX 8–10)

Spiritually inexperienced people despise this teaching. However, God-fearing and anxious consciences find by experience that it brings the greatest consolation. Consciences cannot be set at rest through any works, but only by faith, when they take the sure ground that for Christ's sake they have a gracious God. As Paul teaches, "since we have been justified by faith, we have peace with God" (Romans 5:1). (Ap XX 15–16)

Furthermore, we teach that it is necessary to do good works. This does not mean that we merit grace by doing good works, but because it is God's will (Ephesians 2:10). It is only by faith, and nothing else, that forgiveness of sins is apprehended. The Holy Spirit is received through faith, hearts are renewed and given new affections, and then they are able to bring forth good works. Ambrose says: "Faith is the mother of a good will and doing what is right." Without the Holy Spirit people are full of ungodly desires. They are too weak to do works that are good in God's sight (John 15:5). Besides, they are in the power of the devil, who pushes human beings into various sins, ungodly opinions, and open crimes. We see this in the philosophers, who, although they tried to live an honest life could not succeed, but were defiled with many open crimes. Such is human weakness, without faith and without the Holy Spirit, when governed only by human strength.

Therefore, it is easy to see that this doctrine is not to be accused of banning good works. Instead, it is to be commended all the more because it shows how we are enabled to do good works. For without faith, human nature cannot, in any way, do the works of the First or Second Commandment (1 Corinthians 2:14). Without faith, human nature does not call upon God, nor expect anything from Him, nor bear the cross (Matthew 16:24). Instead, human nature seeks and trusts in human help. So when there is no faith and trust in God, all kinds of lusts and human intentions rule in the heart (Genesis 6:5). This is why Christ says, "Apart from Me you can do nothing" (John 15:5). (AC XX 27–39)

Discussing the Text

92. Why do the confessors begin—again—with the doctrine of justification by grace through faith?

93. Why do God's people do good works? What is the *wrong* motivation for doing "good" works?

94. How do Jesus' words, noted in Article VI, describe the life of a humble disciple?

95. Describe the human heart. What troubles and hardships do we face in life?

96. What kinds of accusations were leveled against the confessors?

97. In what ways does the Augsburg Confession doctrine of good works glorify God?

98. What is the relationship between faith and good works?

99. How only can genuine works be done?

Set Free to Serve

The way the confessors treat the relationship of faith and good works demonstrates how they hold the doctrine of justification to be the chief teaching of the Christian faith. All other doctrines can be correctly understood and taught only when related rightly to the main doctrine. We cannot merit or earn the forgiveness of sins by works that we do. Forgiven in Christ, however, we are freed and strengthened to love and serve God. Only this order of salvation—justification, then sanctification—enables people to do works that please God.

The Apology of the Augsburg Confession

We see that a horrible decree has been prepared against us, which would terrify us still more if we were arguing about doubtful or silly subjects. Our consciences understand that the adversaries condemn the clear truth, whose defense is necessary for the Church and increases Christ's glory. Therefore, we easily look down on the terrors of the world, and we will bear with a strong spirit all suffering for Christ's glory and the Church's benefits. Who would not joyfully die in the confession of these articles, that we receive the forgiveness of sins through faith freely for Christ's sake, and that we do not merit the forgiveness of sins by our works? The consciences of the pious will not have sure enough comfort against the terrors of sin and of death, and against the devil tempting with despair, if they do not know that their confidence lies in the forgiveness of sins freely for Christ's sake. This faith sustains and enlivens hearts in that most violent conflict with despair.

The cause is so worthy that we should refuse no danger. To every one of you who has agreed to our Confession, "Do not yield to the wicked, but, on the contrary, go forward the more boldly." Do not yield when the adversaries, by means of terrors and tortures and punishments, try hard to drive away from you that comfort presented to the entire Church in our article. Those seeking Scripture passages to settle their minds will find them. As the saying goes, at the top of his voice, Paul cries out that sins are freely forgiven for Christ's sake. "It depends on faith," he says, "in order that the promise may rest on grace and be guaranteed" (Romans 4:16; see also Romans 3:24–25). If the promise were to depend upon our works, it would not be sure. If forgiveness of sins were to be given because of our works, when would we know that we had received it? When would a terrified conscience find a work that it would consider enough to reconcile God's anger? (Ap XX 83–87)

Besides, we have shown above well enough that we hold that good works should follow faith. "Do we then overthrow the law?" asks Paul. "On the contrary, we uphold the law" (Romans 3:31), because when we have received the Holy Spirit through faith, the fulfilling of the Law necessarily follows. Patience, chastity, and other fruit of the Spirit gradually grow by this love. (Ap XX 92)

100. In what ways would God's people "joyfully die" for the truth of free salvation in Christ?

101. How do the confessors support their assertion that they do not overthrow the Law?

102. In what ways does salvation by grace *free* you to do good works? *strengthen* you to do good works?

103. "It is God who works in you, both to will and to work for His good pleasure" (Philippians 2:13). How will you celebrate God's working in your life to will and do according to His good purpose?

Good Fruit

Personal Reflection

- Read James 2:14–26. Use the reading to help you understand and practice these words: Faith should produce good fruit and good works, and we must do all such good works as God has commanded.

- Confess your failure to do good works. Ask God to renew your faith and life in Christ and thus empower you to serve in the power and example of Jesus.
- Each morning ask God to enable you "to will and to work for His good pleasure" (Philippians 2:13).

Family Connection

- Share with one another how God's people are confronted with the pitfalls of self-righteousness or apathy.
- Discuss which statement is true: "Justification by faith interferes with good works" or "Justification by faith enables good works."
- Share with one another how the Holy Spirit has recently enabled you to serve others as a person of faith.
- As a family, decide on and do a good work to help someone in need.

Closing Worship

Sing or pray together "Renew Me, O Eternal Light" (*LW* 373).

Renew me, O eternal Light,
And let my heart and soul be bright,
Illumined with the light of grace
That issues from Your holy face.

Create in me a new heart, Lord,
That gladly I obey Your Word.
Let what You will be my desire,
And with new life my soul inspire.

Grant that I only You may love
And seek those things which are above
Till I behold You face to face,
O Light eternal, through Your grace.

For Next Week

Read the selections from Articles VII, VIII, and XV of the Augsburg Confession.

Session 8

The Church: Congregation of Saints

Articles VII, VIII, and XV

Law/Gospel Focus

The Church is the congregation, or assembly, of all believers in Jesus Christ among whom the Gospel is preached in its purity and the Sacraments are administered according to the Gospel. Because of our sinfulness, we often want to preserve and perpetuate our own personal goals and ideas. We stand in need of God's pardon. In Christ, God truly forgives our sins; He strengthens us through the means of grace to live in fellowship and service.

Opening Worship

Read together the following litany based on Ephesians 2.

Leader: For [Christ] Himself is our peace, who has made us both one and has broken down in His flesh the dividing wall of hostility by abolishing the law of commandments and ordinances,

Participants: **that He might create in Himself one new man in place of the two, so making peace, and might reconcile us both to God in one body through the cross, thereby killing the hostility.**

Leader: And He came and preached peace to you who were far off and peace to those who were near.

Participants: **For through Him we both have access in one Spirit to the Father.**

Leader: So then you are no longer strangers and aliens, but you are fellow citizens with the saints and members of the household of God,

Participants: **built on the foundation of the apostles and prophets, Christ Jesus Himself being the cornerstone,**

Leader: in whom the whole structure, being joined together, grows into a holy temple in the Lord.

Participants: **In Him you also are being built together into a dwelling place for God by the Spirit.**

Here Is the Church

What is the *Church?* We use the word in a variety of ways:
- A worldwide fellowship: the Church
- A national denomination: The Lutheran Church—Missouri Synod
- A local congregation: Trinity Lutheran Church

We also refer to the buildings where we worship as *church.* We talk about *going to church.* But which of these uses reflects the teaching of the New Testament? What do the Holy Scriptures teach us about God's purpose and will for His Church? The Augsburg Confession explores these issues in Articles VII, VIII, and XV.

104. How do people view the Church today?

105. In what ways is the Church unique in our world?

106. In what ways do people look to the Church for answers and meaning in life?

Here Is the Steeple

The Augsburg Confession

Our churches teach that one holy Church is to remain forever. The Church is the congregation of saints (Psalm 149:1) in which the Gospel is purely taught and the Sacraments are correctly administered. For the true unity of the Church it is enough to agree about the doctrine of the Gospel and the administration of the Sacraments. It is not necessary that human traditions, that is, rites or ceremonies instituted by men, should be the same everywhere. As Paul says, "One Lord, one faith, one baptism, one God and Father of all" (Ephesians 4:5–6). (AC VII)

Strictly speaking, the Church is the congregation of saints and true believers. However, because many hypocrites and evil persons are mingled within them in this life (Matthew 13:24–30), it is lawful to use Sacraments administered by evil men, according to the saying of Christ, "The scribes and the Pharisees sit on Moses' seat" (Matthew 23:2). (AC VIII 1)

Our churches teach that ceremonies ought to be observed that may be observed without sin. Also, ceremonies and other practices that are profitable for tranquility and good order in the Church (in particular, holy days, festivals, and the like) ought to be observed. Yet, the people are taught that consciences are not to be burdened as though observing such things was necessary for salvation (Colossians 2:16–17). They are also taught that human traditions instituted to make atonement with God, to merit grace, and to make satisfaction for sins are opposed to the Gospel and the doctrine of faith. So vows and traditions concerning meats and days, and so forth, instituted to merit grace and to make satisfaction for sins, are useless and contrary to the Gospel. (AC XV)

Discussing the Text

107. Describe the Church. What does it look like? Where do we find it? What happens there?

108. What, according to the confessors, is sufficient for the true unity of the Church?

109. What is not necessary for the true unity of the Church?

110. Read Matthew 13:24–30. In what ways is Article VIII a commentary on the Lord's parable?

111. Why is it important to uphold the validity of the Sacraments, "even if they are administered by evil men"?

112. When may "rites or ceremonies instituted by men" be observed in the Church? Give some examples.

113. When are "rites or ceremonies instituted by men" not to be observed in the Church? Give some examples.

Open the Door

In these articles on the Church, the confessors challenged the notion that what matters the most are buildings, leadership, and tradition.

They, too, are the Church. By God's design, the Church is the community where the Word is preached, where Baptism is administered in the triune name, where repentant people are absolved, and where God's people eat and drink the body and blood of Christ. What a community!

The Apology of the Augsburg Confession

The Church is not only the fellowship of outward objects and rites, as other governments, but at its core, it is a fellowship of faith and of the Holy Spirit in hearts. Yet this fellowship has outward marks so that it can be recognized. These marks are the pure doctrine of the Gospel and the administration of the Sacraments in accordance with the Gospel of Christ. This Church alone is called Christ's body, which Christ renews, sanctifies, and governs by His Spirit. Paul testifies about this when he says, "And gave Him as head over all things to the Church, which is His body, the fullness of Him who fills all in all" (Ephesians 1:22–23). Those in whom Christ does not act are not the members of Christ. (Ap VII–VIII 5–6)

Hypocrites and wicked people are members of this true Church according to outward rites (titles and offices). Yet, when the Church is defined, it is necessary to define what is the living body of Christ and what is, in name and in fact, the Church. There are many reasons for this. We should understand what chiefly makes us members—living members—of the Church. If we will define the Church only as an outward political order of the good and wicked, people will not understand that Christ's kingdom is righteousness of heart and the gift of the Holy Spirit (Romans 14:17). People will conclude that the Church is only the outward observance of certain forms of worship and rites. Likewise, what difference will there be between the people of the Law and the Church if the Church is only an outward political order? But Paul distinguishes the Church from the people of the Law [Israel] in this way: The Church is a spiritual people. It has not been distinguished from the pagans by civil rites (its polity and civil affairs). Instead, it is God's true people, reborn by the Holy Spirit. Among the people of the Law [Israel], apart from Christ's promise, even the earthly seed had promises about bodily things such as government. Even though the wicked among them were called God's people (because God had separated this earthly seed from other nations by certain outward ordinances and promises), the wicked did not please God (Deuteronomy 7:6–11). But the Gospel brings not merely the shadow of eternal things, but the eternal things themselves: the Holy Spirit and righteousness. By the Gospel we are righteous before God. (Ap VII–VIII 12–15)

According to the Scriptures, we hold that the Church, properly called, is the congregation of saints who truly believe Christ's Gospel and have the Holy Spirit. We confess that in this life many hypocrites and wicked people are mixed in with these. They have the fellowship in outward signs, are members of the Church according to this fellowship in outward signs, and so hold offices in the Church (preach, administer the Sacraments, and bear the title and name of Christians). However, the fact that the Sacraments are administered by the unworthy does not detract from the Sacraments' power. Because of the call of the Church, the unworthy still represent the person of Christ and do not represent their own persons, as Christ testifies, "The one who hears you hears Me" (Luke 10:16). (Even Judas was sent to preach.) When they offer God's Word, when they offer the Sacraments, they offer them in the stead and place of Christ. Those words of Christ teach us not to be offended by the unworthiness of the ministers. (Ap VII–VIII 28)

We cheerfully hold the old traditions made in the Church for the sake of usefulness and peace. We interpret them in a more moderate way and reject the opinion that holds they justify. (Ap XV 38)

But we have an easy and plain case because the adversaries condemn us for teaching that human traditions do not merit the forgiveness of sins. Likewise, the adversaries require universal traditions, as they call them, as necessary for justification. Here we have Paul as a constant champion, who argues everywhere that these ceremonies neither justify nor are they necessary additions to the righteousness of faith. Still, we teach that freedom should be so controlled that the inexperienced may not be offended and, because of freedom's abuse (Romans 14:13–23), may not become more opposed to the true doctrine of the Gospel. Nothing in customary rites should be changed without a reasonable cause. So to nurture unity, old customs that can be kept without sin or great inconvenience should be kept. In this very assembly we have shown well enough that for love's sake we do not refuse to keep adiaphora with others, even though they may be burdensome. We have judged that such public unity, which could indeed be produced without offending consciences, should be preferred. We shall speak about this entire subject later, when we present on vows and Church authority. (Ap XV 50–52)

114. Describe how the Church is a blessing in your life.

115. What assurance do you have when pastors offer you the Word of Christ and the Sacraments?

116. In what ways are traditions of the Church useful and a source of peace and comfort?

117. What are some of the traditions your church has maintained through the years?

118. In what ways is harmony in the Church a blessing?

And See All the People

Personal Reflection

- Reflect on what it means to be a member of Christ's Church. Thank God for the benefits you call to mind.
- Consider how you should think of your relationship to other Christians who live under the Gospel and receive the Sacraments. Consciously live out your response as you are with other Christians during the week.

- Read 1 Thessalonians 1 and discuss how St. Paul understands the Church and what he says about members of the Church. Talk about how Paul's words are helpful to you in recalling and confessing personal sins to God and in rejoicing in God's blessings to you as a member of Christ's Church.

Family Connection

- Share your ideas about what the Church is and what membership in the Church means to your family.
- Have each member of the family write a prayer sentence that uses the word *church*. Gather the prayers and thank God for His rich blessings to you through His Church.
- Talk about church traditions, or usages, that you individually find meaningful. Share why you like the traditions.

Closing Worship

Sing or pray together "I Love Your Kingdom, Lord" (*LW* 296).

I love Your kingdom, Lord,
The place of Your abode;
The Church our blest Redeemer saved
With His own precious blood.

I love Your Church, O God!
Its walls before You stand,
Dear as the apple of Your eye
And graven on Your hand.

Sure as Your truth shall last,
To Zion shall be giv'n
The brightest glories earth can yield
And brighter bliss of heav'n.

For Next Week

Read the selections from Articles IX and XIII of the Augsburg Confession.

Session 9

A Sacramental Means of Grace: Baptism

Articles IX and XIII

Law/Gospel Focus

Because of our sinful nature, we fail to appreciate the Sacraments and we forget the significance of Holy Baptism. We neglect the rich benefits God gives in His gifts. In repentance and faith, we turn to God for pardon and renewal. Through His Word and Sacraments, He forgives us on account of Jesus' great saving work. His Holy Spirit enables us to esteem these life-giving means of grace.

Opening Worship

Read together the following litany based on Titus 3.

Leader: For we ourselves were once foolish, disobedient, led astray, slaves to various passions and pleasures,

Participants: **passing our days in malice and envy, hated by others and hating one another.**

Leader: But when the goodness and loving kindness of God our Savior appeared, He saved us,

Participants: **not because of works done by us in righteousness, but according to His own mercy,**

Leader: by the washing of regeneration and renewal of the Holy Spirit, whom He poured out on us richly through Jesus Christ our Savior,

Participants: **so that being justified by His grace we might become heirs according to the hope of eternal life.**

Good *and* True

"If it *seems* too good to be true, it probably *is*." The Sacraments, like the Gospel we read and hear, almost seem to be too good to be true. But behind ordinary physical elements stands an extraordinary promise from the living God.

What is a sacrament? What is the purpose of a sacrament? What does Baptism, as a sacrament, give us? These are some of the questions the Augsburg Confession answers in Articles IX and XIII.

119. People think God comes to us with His grace in various ways. What are some of their notions?

120. What different opinions do people have about the meaning of Baptism?

More than Signs

The Augsburg Confession

Our churches teach that the Sacraments were ordained, not only to be marks of profession among men, but even more, to be signs and testimonies of God's will toward us. They were instituted to awaken and confirm faith in those who use them. Therefore, we must use the Sacraments in such a way that faith, which believes the promises offered and set forth through the Sacraments, is increased (2 Thessalonians 1:3). (AC XIII 1–2)

Concerning Baptism, our churches teach that Baptism is necessary for salvation (Mark 16:16) and that God's grace is offered through Baptism (Titus 3:4–7). They teach that children are to be baptized (Acts 2:38–39). Being offered to God through Baptism, they are received into God's grace. (AC IX 1–2)

Discussing the Text

121. Describe, in your own words, a sacrament.

122. Why did Christ give sacraments to His Church? In what sense are the sacraments "signs"?

123. What do the Sacraments "require" when properly used?

124. How are the Sacraments "rooted" in the incarnation?

125. Read John 3:1–8. What does Jesus say about the new birth?

126. What does Baptism offer? Explain why Baptism is necessary for *all* people—including children.

127. In what ways is Baptism a personal application of Christ's saving work?

128. Even though Baptism is spoken of as *necessary* for salvation, what can we say about persons who believe in Jesus and are not able to receive Baptism?

God and "Stuff"

God shows His goodness to us by coming to us in the "stuff" of planet earth, where He has placed us to live. He sent His Son to us as a human being. He speaks to us in words we can hear and read. He uses water and bread and wine to come into our lives with His forgiving love and life-changing power. God lets us know where He is and what He has done for us in Christ!

The Apology of the Augsburg Confession

If we call Sacraments "rites that have the command of God, and to which the promise of grace has been added," it is easy to decide what are true Sacraments. For rites instituted by human beings will not be called true Sacraments. For human authority cannot promise grace. Therefore, signs set up without God's command are not sure signs of grace, even though signs perhaps instruct the unlearned or admonish about something. Therefore, *Baptism,* the *Lord's Supper,* and *Absolution* (which is the Sacrament of Repentance) are truly Sacraments. For these rites have God's command and the promise of grace, which is peculiar to the New Testament. When we are baptized, when we eat the Lord's body, when we are absolved, our hearts must be firmly assured that God truly forgives us for Christ's sake. At the same time, by the Word and by the rite, God moves hearts to believe and conceive faith, just as Paul says, "Faith comes from hearing" (Romans 10:17). But just as the Word enters the ear in order to strike our heart, so the rite itself strikes the eye, in order to move the heart. The effect of the Word and of the rite is the same. It has been well said by Augustine that a Sacrament is *a visible Word*, because the rite is received by the eyes and is, as it were, a picture of the Word, illustrating the same thing as the Word. The result of both is the same. (Ap XIII 3–5)

It is more important to understand *how the Sacraments are to be used.* . . . So we teach that in the use of the Sacraments, *faith* should be added. Faith should believe these promises and receive the promised things offered in the Sacrament. The reason is plain and thoroughly grounded. The promise is useless unless it is received by faith. The Sacraments are the signs of the promises. Therefore, faith should be added in the use of the Sacraments. If anyone uses the Lord's Supper, he should use it by faith. This is a Sacrament of the New Testament, as Christ clearly says (Luke 22:20). For this very reason he should be confident that the free forgiveness of sins promised in the New Testament is offered. Let him receive this by faith, let him comfort his alarmed conscience and know that these testimonies are not false. They are as sure as though (and still surer than if) God by a new miracle would declare from heaven that it was His will to grant forgiveness. What advantage would these miracles and promises be to an unbeliever? Here we speak of *special faith* that believes the present promise that the forgiveness of sins is offered. This use of the Sacrament consoles godly and alarmed minds. (Ap XIII 18–22)

We confess that "Baptism is necessary for salvation," that "children are to be baptized," and that the "Baptism of children is not in vain, but is necessary and effective for salvation." Since the Gospel is taught among us purely and diligently . . . it is very certain that the promise of salvation also applies to little children. It does not, however, apply to those who are outside of Christ's Church, where there is neither Word nor Sacraments. Christ's kingdom exists only with the Word and Sacraments. Therefore, it is necessary to baptize little children, that the promise of salvation may be applied to them, according to Christ's command to baptize all nations (Matthew 28:19). Just as in this passage salvation is offered to all, so Baptism is offered to all, to men, women, children, infants. It clearly follows, therefore, that infants are to be baptized, because salvation is offered with Baptism. (Ap IX 51–52)

129. In what ways is it comforting to know that God bestows His extraordinary grace in ordinary ways?

130. How is Absolution, like Baptism and the Lord's Supper, a "genuine" sacrament?

131. Describe how sacraments are "a visible Word."

132. When we use the Sacraments, what are we to believe?

133. Share what Baptism means in your life.

Connected to God

Personal Reflection

- Reflect on the importance of sacraments in your relationship with God. Confess your failure to appreciate these gifts and then take hold of His forgiveness and strength in your life.
- Read Romans 6:1–11. Reflect on St. Paul's words and how Baptism affects your daily life.

Family Connection

- *Luther's Small Catechism with Explanation* (CPH, 1991) defines a sacrament as a "sacred act instituted by God, in which God Himself has joined His Word of promise to a visible element, and by which He offers, gives, and seals the forgiveness of sins earned by Christ" (p. 197). Discuss with one another how these words apply to Holy Baptism and the Lord's Supper.

- Take turns sharing with one another what the Sacraments mean to you for your daily living as Christians.

Closing Worship

Sing or pray together "All Who Believe and Are Baptized" (*LW* 225).

All who believe and are baptized
Shall see the Lord's salvation;
Baptized into the death of Christ,
They are a new creation;
Through Christ's redemption they will stand
Among the glorious heav'nly band
Of ev'ry tribe and nation.

With one accord, O God, we pray,
Grant us Your Holy Spirit;
Help us in our infirmity
Through Jesus' blood and merit;
Grant us to grow in grace each day
By holy Baptism that we may
Eternal life inherit.

For Next Week

Read the selections from Articles X, XXII, and XXIV of the Augsburg Confession.

Session 10

The Holy Supper of Our Lord

Articles X, XXII, and XXIV

Law/Gospel Focus

Jesus has given us the Holy Supper of His body and blood to comfort our consciences and to nurture our faith and life in Him. He bids us to eat and drink for the forgiveness of sins, life, and salvation. Yet we neglect to use the Sacrament regularly, and we often partake with a wrong understanding of His promises. In mercy, our Lord forgives our sins, and He enables us to cherish His Supper where He abides in us and we in Him.

Opening Worship

Read together the following litany based on Psalm 23.

Leader: The LORD is my shepherd; I shall not want.

Participants: **He makes me lie down in green pastures.**

Leader: He leads me beside still waters.

Participants: **He restores my soul. He leads me in paths of righteousness for His name's sake.**

Leader: Even though I walk through the valley of the shadow of death, I will fear no evil,

Participants: **for You are with me; Your rod and Your staff, they comfort me.**

Leader: You prepare a table before me in the presence of my enemies;

Participants: **You anoint my head with oil; my cup overflows.**

81

All: **Surely goodness and mercy shall follow me all the days of my life, and I shall dwell in the house of the LORD forever.**

Holy Unordinary

God graciously comes to us in the water of Baptism to give us the washing of rebirth and renewal in the Holy Spirit. He also comes to us in other things of life. He comes in bread and wine with special gifts.

Justin, an Early Church Father, spoke of these gifts that God has given His people through the years. He wrote, "We do not think this is common bread and drink, but just as Jesus Christ, our Savior, took flesh and blood for our salvation, so this food . . . is the flesh and blood of that incarnate Jesus." In Articles X, XXII, XXIV, the confessors describe the blessings of God in the Lord's Supper.

134. What occasions do people celebrate with dinners or banquets?

135. What does it mean to people to eat and drink together?

Real Presence

The Augsburg Confession

Our churches teach that the body and blood of Christ are truly present and distributed to those who eat the Lord's Supper (1 Corinthians 10:16). They reject those who teach otherwise. (AC X)

The laity are given both kinds in the Sacrament of the Lord's Supper because this practice has the Lord's command, "Drink of it, all of you" (Matthew 26:27). Christ has clearly commanded that all should drink from the cup. . . .

In 1 Corinthians 11:27 Paul cites an example. From this it appears that the whole congregation used both kinds. This practice has remained in the Church for a long time. It is not known when, or by whom, or by whose authority, it was changed. . . . Only a recent custom has changed this. . . . Therefore, if anyone preferred to use both kinds in the Sacrament, they should not have been compelled to do otherwise, as an offense against their conscience. (AC XXII 1–11)

Our churches are falsely accused of abolishing the Mass. The Mass is held among us and celebrated with the highest reverence. Nearly all the usual ceremonies are also preserved, except that the parts sung in Latin are interspersed here and there with German hymns. These have been added to teach the people. For ceremonies are needed for this reason alone, that the uneducated be taught what they need to know about Christ. (AC XXIV 1–3)

It is clear that for a long time the most public and serious complaint among all good people is that the Mass has been made base and profane by using it to gain filthy wealth (1 Timothy 3:3). (AC XXIV 10)

An opinion was added that infinitely increased private Masses. It states that Christ, by His passion, made satisfaction for original sin and instituted the Mass as an offering for daily sins, both venial and mortal. From this opinion has arisen the common belief that the Mass takes away the sins of the living and the dead simply by performing the outward act. . . .

Our teachers have warned that these opinions depart from the Holy Scripture and diminish the glory of the passion of Christ. For Christ's passion was an offering and satisfaction, not only for original guilt, but also for all other sins, as it is written, "We have been sanctified through the offering of the body of Jesus Christ once for all" (Hebrews 10:10). Also, "By a single offering He has perfected for all time those who are being sanctified" (Hebrews 10:14). (AC XXIV 21–27)

Discussing the Text

136. What does Article X confess about the Lord's Supper?

137. What are the gifts (or benefits) Christ bestows in His Supper?

138. What does it mean that "both kinds" are to be given to lay-people in the Sacrament? Why did the confessors insist on this practice?

139. In what ways does changing the Lord's institution burden consciences?

140. What error does Article XXIV reject? Why was this position so offensive to the Gospel?

141. Describe, from the Book of Hebrews, the one sacrifice, for *all* the sins of the world.

142. What is the connection between the Lord's Supper and faith?

His Word Says So

How can this be? reason asks. On the basis of Holy Scripture, we believe that Jesus gives us His true—real—body and blood with bread and wine in His Holy Supper. How this can be is fully known only to God; the Lord's Supper is a great and awesome mystery. Yet what God teaches in His Word is clear: The body and blood of Jesus we receive in the Holy Supper, the body and blood given and shed for us on the cross, are also the body and blood of the exalted and glorified God-man. Exalted and glorified, Jesus is able to be wherever He promises to be and give what He promises to give. He is truly present in His body and blood with bread and wine.

The Apology of the Augsburg Confession

We believe that in the Lord's Supper Christ's body and blood are truly and substantially present and are truly administered with those things that are seen (bread and wine) to those who receive the Sacrament. We constantly defend this belief, as the subject has been carefully examined and considered. Since Paul says, "The bread that we break, is it not a participation in the body of Christ?" (1 Corinthians 10:16), it would follow that if the Lord's body were not truly present, the bread is not a communion of the body, but only of Christ's spirit. (Ap X 54)

We defend the doctrine received in the entire Church. In the Lord's Supper, Christ's body and blood are truly and actually present. They are truly administered with those things that are seen, bread and wine. And we speak of the presence of the living Christ, for we know that "death no longer has dominion over Him" (Romans 6:9). (Ap X 57)

We showed in our Confession our belief that the Lord's Supper does not give grace by the outward act (*ex opere operato*) and that, when applied on behalf of others, alive or dead, it does not merit for them the forgiveness of sins, guilt, or punishment by the outward act. This position is supported by a clear and firm proof. It is impossible to receive the forgiveness of our sins because of our own work by the outward act. The terrors of sin and death must be overcome through faith when we comfort our hearts with the knowledge of Christ and believe that for His sake we are forgiven and that His merits and righteousness are granted to us, "since we have been justified by faith, we have peace" (Romans 5:1). These things are so sure and so firm that they can stand against all the gates of hell (Matthew 16:18). (Ap XXIV 11–12)

A Sacrament is a ceremony or work in which God presents to us what the promise of the ceremony offers. Baptism is not a work that we offer to God. It is a work in which God baptizes us. In other words, a minister baptizes us on God's behalf. God here offers and presents the forgiveness of sins, and so forth, according to the promise "Whoever believes and is baptized will be saved" (Mark 16:16). A sacrifice, on the contrary, is a ceremony or work that we give to God in order to provide Him honor.

Furthermore, there are two kinds of sacrifice and no more. One is the *atoning sacrifice*, that is, a work that makes satisfaction for guilt and punishment. It reconciles God, or reconciles His wrath and merits the forgiveness of sins for others. The other kind is the *eucharistic sacrifice*, which does not merit the forgiveness of sins or reconciliation. It is practiced by those who have been reconciled, so that we may give thanks or return gratitude for the forgiveness of sins that has been received, or for other benefits received. (Ap XXIV 18–19)

In fact there has been only one atoning sacrifice in the world, namely, Christ's death, as the Epistle to the Hebrews teaches, "It is impossible for the blood of bulls and goats to take away sins" (10:4). A little later, of the will of Christ, "By that will we have been sanctified through the offering of the body" (10:10). . . .

Now the rest are *eucharistic* sacrifices, which are called sacrifices of praise (Leviticus 3; 7:11–18; Psalm 56:12). These are the preaching of the Gospel, faith, prayer, thanksgiving, confession, the troubles of saints, yes, all good works of saints. These sacrifices are not satisfactions for those making them, nor can they be applied to others to merit the forgiveness of sins or reconciliation by the outward act (*ex opere operato*). They are made by those who have been reconciled. These are the sacrifices of the New Testament, as Peter teaches, "a holy priesthood, to offer spiritual sacrifices" (1 Peter 2:5). (Ap XXIV 22–25)

143. How do the confessors ground their presentation in the faith and practice of the "entire Church"?

144. The phrase *ex opere operato* means "merely by the work performed." Why did the confessors reject this understanding of the Sacraments?

145. Explain the distinction between atoning and eucharistic sacrifices. Why is this distinction necessary?

146. Share how—and why—Jesus offered the sacrifice that is pleasing to God. What sacrifices can you offer that are pleasing to God?

147. In what ways does the Lord's Supper comfort and encourage you?

148. The Lord's Supper is sometimes called the Eucharist, or the Great Thanksgiving. What mood and attitude do you regularly have as you participate in the Supper?

Taste and See

Personal Reflection

- In your prayers, thank Christ for the Lord's Supper and for specific blessings He gives you in His holy meal.
- Identify sacrifices of praise and thanksgiving, enabled by the Holy Spirit, that you offer during the week.
- Think about the frequency of your reception of the Lord's Supper. Make changes you consider desirable and pleasing to God.

Family Connection

- As a family, discuss what it means that Jesus' body and blood are truly present, distributed, and received in the Lord's Supper.
- Give each family member an opportunity to tell what the Lord's Supper means in his or her life. Talk about the blessings the Holy Supper gives to those who receive our Lord's body and blood in faith.

Closing Worship

Sing or pray together "Lord Jesus Christ, Life-Giving Bread" (*LW* 248).

Lord Jesus Christ, life-giving bread,
May I in grace possess You.
Let me with holy food be fed,
In hunger I address You.
Prepare me well for You, O Lord,
And, humbly by my prayer implored,
Give me Your grace and mercy.

To pastures green, Lord, safely guide,
To restful waters lead me;
Your table well for me provide,
Your wounded hand now feed me.
Though weary, sinful, sick, and weak,
Refuge in You alone I seek,
To share Your cup of healing.

O bread of heav'n, my soul's delight,
For full and free remission
I come with prayer before Your sight
In sorrow and contrition.
Your righteousness, Lord, cover me
That I receive You worthily,
Assured of Your full pardon.

For Next Week

Read Articles XI, XII, and XXV of the Augsburg Confession.

Session 11

Repentance: The Christian Way of Life

Articles XI, XII, and XXV

Law/Gospel Focus

God gives the gifts of repentance and faith to His people. Yet at times we fail to take sin seriously; we neglect to turn to God for mercy and help. We also know the anguish of our sins and search for comfort and pardon. In Christ, God assures us that our sin has been forgiven. He brings us through sorrow to trust in His goodness and renews us to live in our baptismal grace.

Opening Worship

Read together the following litany based on Psalm 130.

Leader: Out of the depths I cry to You, O LORD!

Participants: **O Lord, hear my voice! Let Your ears be attentive to the voice of my pleas for mercy!**

Leader: If You, O LORD, should mark iniquities, O Lord, who could stand?

Participants: **But with You there is forgiveness, that You may be feared.**

Leader: I wait for the LORD, my soul waits, and in His word I hope;

Participants: **my soul waits for the Lord more than watchmen for the morning, more than watchmen for the morning.**

Leader: O Israel, hope in the LORD! For with the LORD there is steadfast love, and with Him is plentiful redemption.

Participants: **And He will redeem Israel from all his iniquities.**

Our Entire Lives

Dr. Luther wrote in his Ninety-five Theses, "When our Lord and Master, Jesus Christ, said 'Repent,' He called for the entire life of believers to be one of repentance."

What is repentance? How does a Christian go about living a life of repentance? These questions are important to everyone committed to living the Christian life. The Augsburg Confession and the Apology provide clear answers in Articles XI, XII, and XXV.

149. What misconceptions do people have about repentance?

150. What reaction do people have to the call to repentance?

Forgiveness Personally Delivered

The Augsburg Confession

Our churches teach that private Absolution should be retained in the churches, although listing all sins is not necessary for Confession. For, according to the Psalm, it is impossible. "Who can discern his errors?" (Psalm 19:12). (AC XI)

Our churches teach that there is forgiveness of sins for those who have fallen after Baptism whenever they are converted. The Church ought to impart Absolution to those who return to repentance (Jeremiah 3:12). Now, strictly speaking, repentance consists of two parts. One part is contrition, that is, terrors striking the conscience through the knowledge of sin. The other part is faith, which is born of the Gospel (Romans 10:17) or the Absolution and believes that for Christ's sake, sins are forgiven. It comforts the conscience and delivers it from terror. Then good works are bound to follow, which are the fruit of repentance (Galatians 5:22–23). (AC XII 1–6)

Confession in the churches is not abolished among us. The body of the Lord is not usually given to those who have not been examined (1 Corinthians 11:27–28) and absolved. The people are very carefully taught about faith in the Absolution. Before, there was profound silence about faith. Our people are taught that they should highly prize the Absolution as being God's voice and pronounced by God's command. The Power of the Keys (Matthew 16:19) is set forth in its beauty. They are reminded what great consolation it brings to anxious consciences and that God requires faith to believe such Absolution as a voice sounding from heaven (e.g., John 12:28–30). They are taught that such faith in Christ truly obtains and receives the forgiveness of sins. (AC XXV 1–4)

Our churches teach that naming every sin is not necessary and that consciences should not be burdened with worry about naming every sin. It is impossible to recount all sins, as Psalm 19:12 testifies: "Who can discern his errors?" Also Jeremiah 17:9, "The heart is deceitful above all things, and desperately sick; who can understand it?" If only sins that can be named are forgiven, consciences could never find peace. For many sins cannot be seen or remembered. . . . Nevertheless, because of the great benefit of Absolution, and because it is otherwise useful to the conscience, Confession is retained among us. (AC XXV 7–13)

Discussing the Text

151. Describe Confession and Absolution. Why is "private Absolution" important for God's people?

152. What, according to the confessors, are the two parts of repentance?

153. How does repentance affect our attitudes? our relationships?

154. What follows repentance? Describe this gift of God.

155. How does Article XII address the following false teachings: Once you're baptized, you cannot sin anymore.

If you sin after Baptism, you cannot be forgiven.

156. What critical part of Absolution do the confessors acknowledge in Article XXV? Why is this so important?

157. Why does Article XXV reject the need to name every sin?

158. What are the use and benefits of private Confession and Absolution?

Comfort for Consciences

From the witness of Holy Scripture, the confessors extol the value of Confession and Absolution for God's people. Through faith, we hear the living Christ speak to our deepest needs today: forgiveness, new life, and salvation. We are richly blessed to know the comfort and hope of the Good News of Jesus.

The Apology of the Augsburg Confession

It is well known that we have made clear and praised the benefit of Absolution and the Power of the Keys. Many troubled consciences have derived comfort from our teaching. They have been comforted after they heard that it is God's command, no, rather the very voice of the Gospel, that we should believe the Absolution and regard it as certain that the forgiveness of sins is freely granted to us for Christ's sake. We should believe that through this faith we are truly reconciled to God. This belief has encouraged many godly minds and, in the beginning, brought Luther the highest praise from all good people. This belief shows consciences sure and firm comfort. (Ap XI 59)

Concerning the *time*, certainly most people in our churches frequently use the Sacraments (Absolution and the Lord's Supper) during the year. Those who teach about the worth and fruit of the Sacraments speak in a way that invites the people to use the Sacraments frequently. There are many writings by our theologians about this subject that the adversaries, if they are good men, will undoubtedly approve and praise. Excommunication is also pronounced against the openly wicked and the haters of the Sacraments. These things are done both according to the Gospel and according to the old canons. A fixed time for Confession is not prescribed because all are not ready in the same way at the same time. Yes, if all were to come at the same time, they could not be heard and instructed in order. (Ap XI 60–62)

We say that contrition is the true terror of conscience, which feels that God is angry with sin and grieves that it has sinned. This contrition takes place when sins are condemned by God's Word. The sum of the preaching of the Gospel is this: to convict of sin; to offer for Christ's sake the forgiveness of sins and righteousness, the Holy Spirit, and eternal life; and that as reborn people we should do good works. So Christ includes the sum of the Gospel when He says, "Repentance and forgiveness of sins should be proclaimed in His name to all nations" (Luke 24:47). (Ap XII 29–30)

As the second part of repentance we add *faith in Christ*. The Gospel, in which the forgiveness of sins is freely promised concerning Christ, should be presented to consciences in these terrors. They should believe that, for Christ's sake, their sins are freely forgiven. This faith cheers, sustains, and enlivens the contrite, according to Romans 5:1, "Since we have been justified by faith, we have peace with God." This faith obtains the forgiveness of sins. It justifies before God, as the same passage testifies, "since we have been justified by faith." This faith shows the distinction between the contrition of Judas and Peter, of Saul and David. The contrition of Judas or Saul (Matthew 27:3–5; 1 Samuel 31:4–6) is useless because faith is not added. Faith grasps the forgiveness of sins, given as a gift for Christ's sake. So the contrition of David or Peter (2 Samuel 12:13; Matthew 26:75) helps because faith, which takes hold of the forgiveness of sins granted for Christ's sake, is added to it. (Ap XII 35–36)

Furthermore, the Power of the Keys administers and presents the Gospel through Absolution, which is the true voice of the Gospel. We also include Absolution when we speak of faith, because "faith comes from hearing," as Paul says in Romans 10:17. When the Gospel is heard and the Absolution is heard, the conscience is encouraged and receives comfort. Because God truly brings a person to life through the Word, the Keys truly forgive sins before God. According to Luke 10:16, "The one who hears you hears Me." Therefore, the voice of the one absolving must be believed no differently than we would believe a voice from heaven. Absolution can properly be called a Sacrament of repentance, as even the more learned scholastic theologians say. Meanwhile, in temptations this faith is nourished in a variety of ways: through the declarations of the Gospel and the use of the Sacraments. For these are signs of the New Testament, that is, signs of the forgiveness of sins. They offer the forgiveness of sins as the words of the Lord's Supper clearly testify, "This is My body, which is given for you. This is the cup of the New Testament," and so on. (See Matthew 26:26, 28.) So faith is conceived and strengthened through Absolution, through the hearing of the Gospel, through the use of the Sacraments, so that it may not give in to the terrors of sin and death while it struggles.

This method of repentance is plain and clear. It increases the worth of the Power of the Keys and of the Sacraments. It illumines Christ's benefit and teaches us to make use of Christ as Mediator and the Atoning Sacrifice. (Ap XII 39–43)

159. In what ways was the "rediscovery" of Absolution a tremendous blessing for the Church of the sixteenth century? for today?

160. What did the Lutheran confessors believe to be at stake in their teaching on Confession and Absolution? Why was it so vital to this gift from God?

161. How are corporate and private Confession and Absolution practiced in your congregation?

162. In what ways does daily repentance "return" you to your Baptism?

163. Share your comfort in receiving the Word and Sacraments in weekly worship.

Freshly Forgiven

Personal Reflection

- Set aside time each day to speak a prayer of repentance to God.
- Make an appointment with your pastor for individual Confession and Absolution.

- Identify the words of absolution in Matthew 9:1–2. Apply these words to your life.

Family Connection

- Thank God together for His gifts of repentance and faith.
- Share with one another your thoughts about how you live together as a family in daily repentance.
- Read 2 Samuel 12:1–14. Discuss what you learned from this portion of Scripture about repentance, confession, and absolution.

Closing Worship

Sing or pray together "To You, Omniscient Lord of All" (*LW* 234).

> To You, omniscient Lord of all,
> With grief and shame I humbly call;
> I see my sins against You, Lord,
> The sins of thought, of deed and word.
> They press me sore; to You I flee:
> O God, be merciful to me!
>
> My Lord and God, to You I pray,
> Oh, cast me not in wrath away;
> Let Your good Spirit ne'er depart,
> But let Him draw to You my heart
> That truly penitent I be:
> O God, be merciful to me!
>
> O Jesus, let Your precious blood
> Be to my soul a cleansing flood.
> Turn not, O Lord, Your guest away,
> But grant that justified I may
> Go to my house, at peace to be:
> O God, be merciful to me!

For Next Week

Read Article XVI of the Augsburg Confession.

Session 12

Civil Government: A Gift of God

Article XVI

Law/Gospel Focus

God has provided civil government for the welfare of all people. Though He calls us to honor and support authority, we often fail to obey His Word and work for the common good in our life's calling. We need God's gracious forgiveness, forgiveness that is freely given for Jesus' sake. Our Savior motivates and enables us to be His light to the world in our callings and communities.

Opening Worship

Read together the following litany based on Romans 13:1–7.

Leader: Let every person be subject to the governing authorities. For there is no authority except from God,

Participants: **and those that exist have been instituted by God.**

Leader: Therefore, whoever resists the authorities resists what God has appointed, and those who resist will incur judgment.

Participants: **For rulers are not a terror to good conduct, but to bad.**

Leader: Lord God, forgive our failures to honor authority.

Participants: **Forgive us when we despise the leaders and officials You place over us.**

Leader: By the power of Your Holy Spirit, help us to honor, serve, and obey them;

Participants: **help us to hold them in love and esteem; through Jesus Christ, our Lord. Amen.**

We the People

People have different attitudes toward civil government. There are those who think of civil government as evil and as something to be avoided and not trusted. There are others who look to civil government to solve all human problems; they give it unquestioned support.

What is your attitude toward the political order? Where did the whole idea of civil government come from? Can Christians, in good conscience, be part of government? What are our duties toward government? These are some of the questions that the confessors examined in Article XVI.

164. What attitudes toward government do you regularly see and hear?

165. In what ways have attitudes toward authority changed in your lifetime?

Good Order

The Augsburg Confession

Our churches teach that lawful civil regulations are good works of God. They teach that it is right for Christians to hold political office, to serve as judges, to judge matters by Imperial laws and other existing laws, to impose just punishments, to engage in just wars, to serve as soldiers, to make legal contracts, to hold property, to take oaths when required by the magistrates, for a man to marry a wife, or a woman to be given in marriage (Romans 13; 1 Corinthians 7:2).

Our churches condemn [those] who forbid these political offices to Christians. They also condemn those who do not locate evangelical perfection in the fear of God and in faith, but place it in forsaking political offices. For the Gospel teaches an eternal righteousness of the heart (Romans 10:10). At the same time, it does not require the destruction of the civil state or the family. The Gospel very much requires that they be preserved as God's ordinances and that love be practiced in such ordinances. Therefore, it is necessary for Christians to be obedient to their rulers and laws. The only exception is when they are commanded to sin. Then they ought to obey God rather than men (Acts 5:29). (AC XVI)

Discussing the Text

166. Explain the statement "God instituted and ordained all government and established rules and laws."

167. Why did God institute and ordain government?

168. Describe the ways Christians may be involved in civil government today.

169. In the sixteenth century, what was the attitude of some Christians toward government? toward involvement in civic affairs?

170. In what ways does Article XVI affirm Christian homes and families?

171. What is "evangelical perfection" for Christians? Relate this to Law and Gospel.

172. What do the confessors mean by "the Gospel teaches an eternal righteousness of the heart"?

173. What are our obligations—as God's people—to the state? When are these obligations set aside?

Two Kingdoms

God rules in two ways: in the spiritual realm and in the secular, or political, sphere. God rules in both ways for our good and the good of all people. This means Christians live in *two kingdoms.* We are to live faithfully in both to receive the blessings God offers in each and to help others receive the gifts of God for their spiritual and physical well-being.

The Apology of the Augsburg Confession

In [Article XVI of the Augsburg Confession] we have confessed that it is lawful for the Christian to hold public office, sit in judgment, determine matters by the imperial laws and other laws currently in force, set just punishments, engage in just wars, act as a soldier, make legal contracts, hold property, take an oath (when public officials require it), and contract marriage. Finally, we have confessed that legitimate public ordinances are good creations of God and divine ordinances, which a Christian can safely use. This entire topic *about the distinction between the spiritual kingdom of Christ and a political kingdom* has been explained in the literature of our writers. Christ's kingdom is spiritual (John 18:36). This means that the knowledge of God, the fear of God and faith, eternal righteousness, and eternal life begin in the heart. Meanwhile, Christ's kingdom allows us outwardly to use legitimate political ordinances of every nation in which we live, just as it allows us to use medicine or the art of building, or food, drink, and air. Neither does the Gospel offer new laws about the public state, but commands that we obey present laws, whether they have been framed by heathens or by others. It commands that in this obedience we should exercise love. (Ap XVI 53–55)

The Gospel does not introduce laws about the public state, but is the forgiveness of sins and the beginning of a new life in the hearts of believers. Besides, the Gospel not only approves outward governments, but also subjects us to them (Romans 13:1). In a similar way we have been necessarily placed under the laws of seasons, the changes of winter and summer, as divine ordinances. The Gospel forbids private remedy. Christ instills this often so that the apostles do not think they should seize the governments from those who held otherwise. (Ap XVI 58–59)

It is also a most empty myth that Christian perfection consists in not holding property. For Christian perfection does not consist in contempt for public ordinances, but in the inclinations of the heart, in great fear of God, and in great faith. Abraham, David, and Daniel, even in great wealth and while exercising public power, were no less perfect than any hermits. (Ap XVI 61)

There are countless discussions about contracts. Good consciences can never be satisfied about them unless they know the rule that it is lawful for a Christian to make use of public ordinances and laws. This rule protects consciences. It teaches that contracts are lawful before God just to the extent that the public officials or laws approve them. (Ap XVI 64)

174. What aspects of the Lutheran teaching on government and political order are most relevant to our day?

175. Describe the distinctions between the two kingdoms. How does each kingdom apply to your life?

176. In what ways does the Gospel "approve" and "subject us to" government?

177. "We can and should obey just laws formulated by non-Christians." Use Article XVI to defend this principle.

178. How can God's people contribute to good order in society?

Good Citizens

Personal Reflection

- As you read magazines and newspapers, watch TV, and surf the Internet during the week, note what benefits good government and civic authority have provided for you and other citizens.
- Identify ways in which you might participate more fully in the government of your town or city, state, or nation. Initiate action to implement your resolves.
- If and when the time should come that you believe the government is asking you to do something you cannot in good conscience do as a Christian, how will you respond?

Family Connection

- Together, put into action St. Paul's words in 1 Timothy 2:1–3.
- Share how authority promotes stability and order in your home, neighborhood, and community.
- Write a letter or note of appreciation to a local or state law-enforcement official.

Closing Worship

Sing or pray together "Lord, While for Humankind We Pray" (*LW* 502).

> Lord, while for humankind we pray
> Of ev'ry clime and coast,
> Lord, hear us for our native land,
> The land we love the most!
>
> Oh, guard our shores from ev'ry foe,
> With peace our borders bless,
> With prosp'rous times our cities crown,
> Our fields with plenteousness!
>
> Unite us in the sacred love
> Of all that's good and true;
> And let our hills and valleys shout
> Their songs, all praising You.
>
> Lord of the nations, thus to You
> Our country we commend.
> Oh, be her refuge and her trust,
> Her everlasting friend.

For Next Week

Read Article XVII of the Augsburg Confession.

Session 13

The Return of Christ

Article XVII

Law/Gospel Focus

God offers us a sure and certain hope: Jesus will return, raise up all the dead, and give us and all believers eternal life. Yet we sometimes live as though we have no hope; we fear the present, the future, and above all, death. God's forgiveness, however, is His ongoing gift to His people in Christ. In Jesus' death and resurrection, we find lasting hope and an eternal perspective for our lives.

Opening Worship

Read together the following litany based on 1 Peter 1:3–9.

Leader: Blessed be the God and Father of our Lord Jesus Christ!

Participants: **According to His great mercy, He has caused us to be born again to a living hope through the resurrection of Jesus Christ from the dead,**

Leader: to an inheritance that is imperishable, undefiled, and unfading, kept in heaven for you,

Participants: **who by God's power are being guarded through faith for a salvation ready to be revealed in the last time.**

Leader: In this you rejoice, though now for a little while, if necessary, you have been grieved by various trials,

Participants: **so that the tested genuineness of your faith—more precious than gold that perishes though it is tested by fire—**

Leader: may be found to result in praise and glory and honor at the revelation of Jesus Christ.

Participants: **Though you have not seen Him, you love Him.**

Leader: Though you do not now see Him, you believe in Him and rejoice with joy that is inexpressible and filled with glory,

Participants: **obtaining the outcome of your faith, the salvation of your souls.**

Key to the Future

All over the world people are asking, "What does the future hold?" Some believe the world will end soon. Some believe that human life will go on with little or no change.

Christians too have different views on the end of time. The key, however, is to ask, "What does God say in His Word?" The confessors answer this question in Article XVII.

179. What views are current on the future? on Jesus' return?

180. How do people react to the Last Day?

Our Returning King

The Augsburg Confession

Our churches teach that at the end of the world Christ will appear for judgment and will raise all the dead (1 Thessalonians 4:13–5:2). He will give the godly and elect eternal life and everlasting joys, but He will condemn ungodly people and the devils to be tormented without end (Matthew 25:31–46).

Our churches condemn [those] who think that there will be an end to the punishments of condemned men and devils.

Our churches also condemn those who are spreading certain . . . opinions, that before the resurrection of the dead the godly shall take possession of the kingdom of the world, the ungodly being everywhere suppressed. (AC XVII)

Discussing the Text

181. Describe, in your own words, the sure and certain hope of God's people at the end of time.

182. What does the final judgment hold for believers? for unbelievers? for Satan and all evil forces?

183. Why, in your view, would the confessors include an article on the return of Christ?

184. In what ways do people today deny the reality of hell and punishment?

185. In what ways do people today hold false opinions on the millennium and our earthly kingdom of Christ?

186. How does St. Paul hold high the Gospel as he describes the Lord's return in glory to the Thessalonians?

But we do not want you to be uninformed, brothers, about those who are asleep, that you may not grieve as others do who have no hope. For since we believe that Jesus died and rose again, even so, through Jesus, God will bring with Him those who have fallen asleep. For this we declare to you by a word from the Lord, that we who are alive, who are left

107

until the coming of the Lord, will not precede those who have fallen asleep. For the Lord Himself will descend from heaven with a cry of command, with the voice of an archangel, and with the sound of the trumpet of God. And the dead in Christ will rise first. Then we who are alive, who are left, will be caught up together with them in the clouds to meet the Lord in the air, and so we will always be with the Lord. Therefore encourage one another with these words.

Now concerning the times and the seasons, brothers, you have no need to have anything written to you. For you yourselves are fully aware that the day of the Lord will come like a thief in the night. While people are saying, "There is peace and security," then sudden destruction will come upon them as labor pains come upon a pregnant woman, and they will not escape.

But you are not in darkness, brothers, for that day to surprise you like a thief. For you are all children of light, children of the day. We are not of the night or of the darkness. So then let us not sleep, as others do, but let us keep awake and be sober. (1 Thessalonians 4:13–5:6)

187. What does Paul say about the "times and seasons" of the second coming?

188. What ministry does St. Paul invite us to give to one another? When is this ministry especially needed?

Endless Joy

The Apology of the Augsburg Confession

In [Article XVII of the Augsburg Confession] we confess that Christ will appear at the consummation of the world. He will raise up all the dead and will give eternal life and eternal joys to the godly (2 Timothy 4:8), but He will condemn the ungodly to endless punishment with the devil (Matthew 25:46). (Ap XVII)

189. Describe how the promise of Christ's return brings joy into your life today.

190. How did Christ show Himself alive after His resurrection? How does His resurrection assure us of our own resurrection?

191. Who among your family and friends needs to hear about Jesus and His forgiving love?

Sharing Hope

To Do This Week

- Meditate on St. Paul's words in 1 Corinthians 15. What comfort do you have from God's promise of resurrection and eternal life?
- Ask God to strengthen your "Last-Days" hope so that you have greater endurance in difficult times and encouragement in the face of death.

- If and when you have opportunity, comfort and encourage a discouraged Christian with the hope of Christ's return and the blessings He will bring.

Family Connection

- Identify from your reading, TV watching, and Internet surfing some of the things people are saying about the end of the world. Discuss these views in the light of Scripture and the Augsburg Confession.
- Think of someone who needs the encouragement of the blessings of Christ's return. Make a family visit and/or send a card or note of hope and reassurance.
- Share with one another what it means to you for your daily living that Jesus will come again, raise up the dead, and give eternal life and everlasting joy to all believers.

Closing Worship

Sing or pray together "Lord, Keep Us Steadfast in Your Word" (*LW* 334).

> Lord, keep us steadfast in Your Word;
> Curb those who by deceit or sword
> Would wrest the kingdom from Your Son
> And bring to nought all He has done.
>
> Lord Jesus Christ, Your pow'r make known,
> For You are Lord of lords alone;
> Defend Your holy Church that we
> May sing Your praise triumphantly.
>
> O Comforter of priceless worth,
> Send peace and unity on earth;
> Support us in our final strife
> And lead us out of death to life.